Billy Sunday Speaks

13

134

127 - nothing

snl
189

86

167
168
169

152

170
171
173
175

Billy Sunday Speaks

Introduction by
Oral Roberts

Edited by
Karen Gullen

1970
CHELSEA HOUSE PUBLISHERS
NEW YORK

CONTENTS

Billy Sunday—The Man

ORAL ROBERTS

very week at Oral Roberts University in Tulsa, Oklahoma, KORU, the University's FM radio station, carries the program of the Pacific Garden Mission. I am reminded each time I hear this program of the Mission's 85-year-old history of reaching out to the down-and-outers of America.

One of those down-and-outers reached in the Mission's early days was Billy Sunday. When first confronted by Christ, he was a drinking, cursing, rough-and-tumble professional baseball player, but he was soon transformed into one of the world's outstanding soul-winners.

We of the twentieth century owe a great deal to Billy Sunday, for as the century opened he spearheaded a spiritual renewal in the religious life of America. A lethargy and falling away among churchgoers, a materialistic emphasis in the nation, as well as a deepening religious skepticism were assaulting the Church. A champion of faith was needed —a man for the hour.

God's man for that hour was none other than Billy Sunday. Since the day he met Christ at the Mission in 1886, Sunday had been preparing for the special task God had in store for him.

As a young Christian he started out working with the Y.M.C.A.—this was when evangelism was an important part of the Y's work. A few years later he was recommended by his Y associates to assist as an "advance man" for the Rev. J. Wilbur Chapman's evangelistic meetings. It was there that he gained experience in organization and planning for successful evangelistic ventures. Then, when Chapman suddenly accepted a call to the pastorate and cancelled his meetings, Sunday, at the insistence of those who had scheduled a revival for Chapman, agreed to fill in. From then on, he was on his own—in God's hands.

By 1900 the larger role that God had for Sunday began to emerge.

The big cities began calling for his ministry. Soon the response to his meetings was in the thousands. The results more than offset any criticism of his unorthodox style and message. The controversy surrounding him only aided in reaching more and more people. His meetings became front page news. Leading newspaper reporters covered his services and told of his sermons. His friendship was coveted by the rich and important. Political figures were on a first-name basis with him. Conversions during his revivals ran into the tens of thousands. In New York alone, nearly 100,000 were won to Christ.

The two decades from 1900-1920 were a religious phenomenon to the skeptic—a transfusion of power for the Church. Those years of Sunday's life and ministry can teach us a great deal.

First, they tell us that there can be no question of Billy Sunday's commitment to Christ. His commitment was not something that had happened years before, but it was a reality he kept alive through constant witnessing and service to others.

For Billy Sunday learned the meaning of sowing and reaping. And this is really what Christian faith is all about. It is giving of yourself— your time, your talents as seed planted—and then expecting God to bring the results. Billy planted the seed and reaped a harvest of souls won to Christ.

Second, Billy Sunday paid his bills. He was a good businessman. Few things can be more damaging to a minister than carelessness about personal finances. This is especially true of evangelists.

I remember during the early days of my own ministry I was in a meeting in Chanute, Kansas. I was praying hard, preaching hard—and the financial needs of the meeting were going hard! In fact, the offerings were falling far short of what was needed. One night near the end of the meeting when the offering was taken and counted, I realized that I was not able to pay the rent for the auditorium. Something went all over me. Suddenly I felt I couldn't go out and face the people, much less preach and pray for them.

Just before the time for me to enter the pulpit I told my brother, Vaden, that I wasn't preaching—that in fact, I was going home. When Vaden related this to my wife, Evelyn, she did something she had never done before nor has since. She went to the platform and told the people of the need. Then, she passed a hat among the people. Returning to me she said, "Oral Roberts, God called you to this ministry. You've got to go preach and pray for those people."

Ever since I met Evelyn I knew that God had given her to me. She proved it that night. Without saying a word I went out and preached and prayed. Souls were saved, and people were healed in body, mind, and soul. *And*, the bills were paid. In the twenty-three years since, no matter where we've gone, we have never left an unpaid bill. Neither has our organization ever been late in meeting its obligations.

I'm thankful for the example that Billy Sunday left for all of us ministers and evangelists. It's one we should be careful to follow.

Third, Billy Sunday was not afraid to use new and untried methods to reach the people. For some reason there seems to be a timidity among God's people to try the unconventional. We marry our methods and think because we've always done it a certain way that there is only one way God can work. But not Billy Sunday. The tabernacles Sunday had built for his meetings were different. The sawdust on the floors to muffle the sound of shuffling feet was different. The organization, the planning and preparation, the service itself—its music, sermon and style— all were different.

I think every minister is faced with the dilemma of whether or not to try the untried, the unusual, the different. We become concerned about what our congregation or fellow ministers will think. In fact, the structure and methods of promotion in our denominations almost demand that a minister not be unusual or different.

Before I entered this ministry, while pastoring a small church in Enid, Oklahoma, I wrestled with the same problem. I wanted to do what I felt God had called me to do, yet I had all the doubts and insecurities about trying something new that every pastor has. One day, though, the situation came to a peak. A clear witness was called for. It would mean a ministry that was different. Then God spoke to my heart and solved the dilemma. He said, "Son, don't be like others. Be like Jesus . . ."

That's the command God calls all of us to obey. To be like his Son. To preach, to teach, to pray, to give. To identify with people in need and give them Jesus.

Billy Sunday was God's man, in God's time, at God's place. He had a national impact and became virtually a prophet to the nation. His uncompromising message of judgment and hope filled a void in America. Phenomenally, his success came before radio or television.

From the perspective of this hour we could perhaps find weaknesses. Yet, his ministry stands on its results—the fruit of his labors. By this standard each man is ultimately judged. And on that score Billy Sunday was without peer—a 20th Century pioneer in mass evangelism.

I commend this book of Sunday's sermons to you. The language, the illustrations, the unusual style combine to help you relive with Sunday an era when God brought a great revival to America.

May Jesus of Nazareth bless this book to your heart and life—and He will!

Tulsa, Oklahoma
September 1970

William Ashley Sunday

A Biographical Sketch

illiam Ashley Sunday was born in Ames, Iowa on November 19, 1862. His father, a Union soldier, had been killed in the Civil War two months before. As a result, Billy's childhood had few roots. The young boy was shifted about—from the log-cabin home of his birth, to a soldiers' orphanage, and eventually to the farm of his maternal grandfather.

Sports were Billy's first love. Always an agile athlete, one who could run the hundred-yard dash in ten seconds, Billy was a natural on the baseball diamond and played for several of the local teams. He was quickly discovered by baseball great "Pop" Anson, who signed him to the Chicago White Stockings as a center-fielder in 1883.

As a baseball player—his career lasted from 1883 to 1891—Billy Sunday became noted for his speed and fielding talents. He allegedly was the first to run the bases in fourteen seconds, a feat that only a few in baseball history have been able to duplicate. His ability with the bat, however, was something else. Although playing in an era when batting averages often soared around the .400 figure, Billy's lifetime mark was but .254. Considering his blazing speed, this low figure suggests a hitting skill which, speaking graciously, must have bordered on the nonexistent In fact, he struck out the first thirteen times to the plate, prompting the now-famous remark of one observer, "If only he could steal first." Nevertheless, he was a favorite with the fans, who delighted at his madcap, mercurial dashes around the bases.

But, if William Ashley Sunday were alive today, he would probably say that his life began not in an old Iowa log cabin, but at the Pacific Garden Mission in Chicago one day in 1886. It was there that Billy

Sunday, at age twenty-four and without real personal direction, took his stand for Christ. On that spring day he chanced to find the Mission holding a Sunday afternoon street revival. After the service, the minister noticed that Billy had been moved, and he invited him to the Mission house—his conversion followed.

Billy Sunday continued his baseball career for another five years, but in 1891 he left the sport to join the Y.M.C.A. as an assistant secretary. During his three-year association with that organization he worked with evangelist Dr. J. Wilbur Chapman, who gave him many opportunities to develop his speaking abilities. Billy Sunday received his first preaching invitation in 1896 from a Church in Garner, Iowa, and thus began a career which lasted until his death in 1935.

Billy Sunday's success was immediate, and the evangelist realized that he could be reaching thousands more if he had larger facilities. The idea of a tabernacle suggested itself, and the first Sunday tabernacle was built in Perry, Iowa—one of many to grow up all over the country in the 1900's.

Billy's athletic abilities were well-suited to his new calling. On the stump, he was a commanding presence. One minute he would be motionless, the next the air would resound with the terrific clap of his large hands. Then his fist would come crashing down on a chair with such force that the audience would shudder. Above all, he was unpredictable. On occasion he would promenade across the platform and suddenly fall flat on his face—and continue with his sermon! Perhaps some thought that these physical exertions were all a "put on," a ploy to attract people to the meetings. True, his forceful, colorful demonstrations did attract people, and if he had not used his antics he probably would not have enjoyed such unprecedented success. In retrospect, though, Billy's gyrations probably were as spontaneous as the rapid bursts of speed he used in stealing a base.

Yet, Billy Sunday used the simplest of speech. He called things by their right names, even if in doing so, he had to use words that burned and blistered. He rarely read from a prepared text—a photographic memory enabled him to memorize his sermons rapidly. He used everyday illustrations; in fact, he would often purposely use common slang to make his point. Yet to Billy the message was the same as that preached by Jesus, and the people respected him all the more for it.

Throughout his career, Billy Sunday encountered opposition, ridicule and slander, but he never wavered in his convictions. He hated sin, the devil, vanity and anything said against Jesus Christ. He believed in the holiness of motherhood, the veneration of hard labor, the godliness of Christiandom. But his favorite topic or target, at home or on the pulpit, was alcohol—"booze" as he called it. Indeed, his most famous and perhaps his longest sermon (included in this collection) is on the evil "spirits."

The Sunday staff consisted of about eight dedicated workers who were responsible for scheduling the revivals, erecting the tabernacles, and collecting the donations. Usually, the town membership of the various churches financially supported the Sunday campaigns. For many years, however, Billy personally assumed a larger share of the "crusade" expenses. Homer Rodeheaver, a close friend of Billy Sunday's and a former associate, estimated that at the height of his career, Billy accumulated a million dollars in free-will offerings from every part of the country. The Sunday estate was probated at $50,000.

If newspaper coverage and magazine accounts are a judge, Billy Sunday, without a doubt, was by far the most popular evangelical minister of his day. Through his work, in an era before television, he paved the way for such evangelists as Billy Graham and Oral Roberts. His Biblical guideline, which he repeated over and over, was a line from Timothy: "Study to show thyself approved unto God, a workman that needeth not to be ashamed, rightly dividing the word of truth."

During his forty-year ministry, Billy Sunday preached to more than a hundred million people—grasping the hands of all races, creeds and classes. By 1935, the year of his death, he had been credited with almost a quarter of a million conversions. This collection of his sermons is a testimony to Billy Sunday's Christian gianthood—a book of his words that he might place on his mantelpiece in Heaven.

KAREN GULLEN

New York City
August, 1970

Sermons

A Plain Speech

The hour is come; come for something else. It has come for plainness of speech on the part of the preacher. If you have anything to antagonize, out with it; specify sins and sinners. You can always count on a decent public to right a wrong, and any public that won't right a wrong is a good one to get out of.

Charles Finney went to Europe to preach, and in London a famous free-thinker's wife went to hear him. The free-thinker's wife noticed a great change in him; he was more kind, more affectionate, more affable, less abusive and she said, "I know what is the matter with you; you have been to hear that man from America preach." And he said, "Wife, that is an insult; that man Finney don't preach; he just makes plain what the other fellows preach." Now the foremost preacher of his day was Paul. What he preached of his day was not so much idealism as practicality; not so much theology, homiletics, exegesis or didactics, but a manner of life. I tell you there was no small fuss about his way of teaching. When Paul was on the job the devil was awake. There is a kind of preaching that will never arouse the devil.

"He that believeth not is condemned already." He that has not believed in Jesus Christ, the only begotten son of God, is condemned where he sits.

Too much of the preaching of today is too nice; too pretty; too dainty; it does not kill. Too many sermons are just given for literary excellence of the production. They get a nice adjective or noun, or pronoun—you cannot be saved by grammar. A little bit of grammar is all right, but don't be a big fool and sit around and criticize because the preacher gets a word wrong—if you do that your head is filled with buck oysters and sawdust, if that is all that you can use it for.

They've been crying peace. There is no peace. Some people won't come to hear me because they are afraid to hear the truth. They want deodorized, disinfected sermons. They are afraid to be stuck over the edge of the pit and get a smell of the brimstone. You can't get rid of sin as long as you treat it as a cream puff instead of a rattlesnake. You can't brush sin away with a feather duster. Go ask the drunkard who has been made sober whether he likes "Bill." Go ask the girl who was dragged from the quagmire of shame and restored to her mother's arms whether she likes "Bill." Go ask the happy housewife who gets the pay envelope every Saturday night instead of its going to the filthy saloonkeeper whether she's for "Bill." Some people say, "Oh, he's sensational." Nothing would be more sensational than if some of you were suddenly to become decent. I would rather be a guide-post than a tombstone.

I repeat that everybody who is decent or wants to be decent, will admire you when you preach the truth, although you riddle them when you do it. The hour is come, my friend. The hour is come to believe in a revival. Some people do not believe in revivals; neither does the devil; so you are like your daddy.

I can see those disciples praying, and talking and having a big time. There are many fool short-sighted ministers who are satisfied if they can only draw a large crowd. Some are as crazy after sensations as the yellowest newspaper that ever came off the press. That's the reason we have these sermons on "The Hobble Skirt" and "The Merry Widow Hat" and other such nonsensical tommyrot. If there were not so many March-hare sort of fellows breaking into pulpits you would have to sweat more and work harder. There are some of you that have the devil in you. Maybe you don't treat your wife square. Maybe you cheat in your weights. Get rid of the devil. What does it matter if you pack a church to the roof if nothing happens to turn the devil pale? What is the use of putting chairs in the aisles and out the doors?

The object of the Church is to cast out devils.

The devil has more sense than lots of little preachers. I have been unfortunate enough to know D.D.'s and LL.D.'s sitting around whittling down the doctrine of the personality of the devil to as fine a point as they know how. You are a fool to listen to them. The devil is no fool, he is no four-flusher. He said to Christ: "If you are a God, act like it; if you are a man, and believe the Scriptures, act as one who believes."

John the Baptist wasn't that kind of a preacher. Jesus Christ wasn't that kind of a preacher. The apostles weren't that kind of preachers—except old Judas. John the Baptist opened the Bible right in the middle and preached the word of God just as he found it, and he didn't care whether the people liked it or not. That wasn't his business. I tell you, John the Baptist stirred up the devil. If any minister doesn't believe in a personal devil it's because he has never preached a sermon on repentance, or he'd have heard him roar. Yes, sir. If there's anything that will make the devil roar it is a sermon on repentance.

You can preach sociology, or psychology, or any other kind of ology, but if you leave Jesus Christ out of it you hit the toboggan slide to hell.

I'll preach against any minister who is preaching false doctrines. I don't give a rap who he is. I'll turn my guns loose against him, and don't you forget that. Any man who is preaching false doctrines to the people and vomiting out false doctrines to them will hear from me. I want to say that the responsibility for no revivals in our cities and towns has got to be laid at the doors of the ministry. Preachers sit fighting their sham battles of different denominations, through their cussedness, inquiring into fol-da-rol and tommyrot, and there sits in the pews of the church that miserable old scoundrel who rents his property out for a saloon and is going to hell; and that other old scoundrel who rents his houses for houses of ill fame and is living directly on the proceeds of prostitution, and he doesn't preach against it. He is afraid he will turn the men against him. He is afraid of his job. They are a lot of back-sliders and the whole bunch will go to hell together. They are afraid to come out against it.

I'll tell you what's the matter. Listen to me. The Church of God has lost the spirit of concern today largely because of the ministry—that's what's the matter with them. I'll allow no man or woman to go beyond me in paying tribute to culture. I don't mean this miserable "dog" business, shaking hands with two fingers. The less brains some people have the harder they try to show you that they have some, or think they have. I allow no man to go beyond me in paying tribute to real, genuine culture, a tribute to intellectual greatness; but when a man stands in the pulpit to preach he has got to be a man of God. He has got to speak with the passion for souls. If you sleep in the time of a revival God Almighty will wake you up.

There are lots of preachers who don't know Jesus. They know about him, but they don't know him. Experience will do more than forty million theories. I can experiment with religion just the same as I can with water. No two knew Him exactly alike, but all loved Him. All would have something to say.

Now for you preachers. When a man prays "Thy Kingdom Come" he will read the Bible to find out the way to make it come. The preacher who prays "Thy Kingdom Come" will not get all his reading from the news books or from the magazines. He will not try to please the highbrows and in pleasing them miss the masses. He will not try to tickle the palates of the giraffes and then let the sheep starve. He will put his cookies on the lower shelf. He will preach in a language that the commonest laborer can understand.

One of the prolific sources of unbelief and backsliding today is a bottle-fed church, where the whole membership lets the preacher do the studying of the Bible for them. He will go to the pulpit with his mind full of his sermon and they will come to the church with their minds filled with society and last night's card-playing, beer-and-wine-drinking and novel-reading party and will sit there half asleep. Many a preacher reminds me of a great big nursing bottle, and there are two hundred or three hundred rubber tubes, with nipples on the end, running into the mouths of two hundred or three hundred or four hundred great big old babies with whiskers and breeches on, and hair pins stuck in their heads and rats in their hair, sitting there, and they suck and draw from the preacher. Some old sister gets the "Amusement" nipple in her mouth and it sours her stomach, and up go her heels and she yells. Then the preacher has to go around and sing psalms to that big two-hundred-and-fifty-pound baby and get her good-natured so that she will go back to church some day.

By and by some old whisky-voting church member gets the "Temperance" nipple in his mouth and it sours his stomach and up go his heels and he lets out a yell, throws his hands across his abdominal region, and the preacher says, "Whatever is the matter? If I hit you any place but the heart or the head I apologize." The preacher has to be wet nurse to about two hundred and fifty big babies that haven't grown an inch since they came into the church.

One reason why some preachers are not able to bring many sinners to repentance is because they preach of a God so impotent that he can only throw down card houses when all the signs are right! They decline to magnify his power for fear they will overdo it! And if they accidentally make a strong assertion as to his power, they immediately neutralize it by "as it were," or "in a measure, perhaps!"

You make a man feel as though God was stuck on him and you'll be a thirty-third degree sort of a preacher with that fellow.

If some preachers were as true to their trust as John the Baptist, they might be turned out to grass, but they'd lay up treasures for themselves in heaven.

Clergymen will find their authority for out-of-the-ordinary methods in the lowering of a paralytic through a roof, as told of in the Bible. If that isn't sensationalism, then trot some out.

If God could convert the preachers the world would be saved. Most of them are a lot of evolutionary hot-air merchants.

We've got churches, lots of them. We've got preachers, seminaries, and they are turning out preachers and putting them into little theological molds and keeping them there until they get cold enough to practice preaching.

The reason some ministers are not more interested in their work is because they fail to realize that theirs is a God-given mission.

We've got a bunch of preachers breaking their necks to please a lot of old society dames.

Some ministers say, "If you don't repent, you'll die and go to a place, the name of which I can't pronounce." I can. You'll go to hell.

There is not a preacher on earth that can preach a better gospel than "Bill." I'm willing to die for the Church. I'm giving my life for the Church.

Your preachers would fight for Christ if some of you fossilated, antiquated old hypocrites didn't snort and snarl and whine.

A godless cowboy once went to a brown-stone church—with a high-toned preacher—I am a half-way house between the brown-stone church and the Salvation Army. They are both needed and so is the half-way house. Well, this fellow went to one of these brown-stone churches and after the preacher had finished the cowbody thought he had to go up and compliment the preacher, as he saw others doing, and so he sauntered down the aisle with his sombrero under his arm, his breeches stuck in his boots, a bandana handkerchief around his neck, his gun and bowie knife in his belt, and he walked over and said: "Hanged if I didn't fight shy of you fellows—but I'll tell you I sat here and listened to you for an hour and you monkeyed less with religion than any fellow I ever heard in my life." They have taken away the Lord and don't know where to find him.

You must remember that Jesus tells us to shine for God. The trouble with some people and preachers is that they try to shine rather than letting their light shine. Some preachers put such a big capital "I" in front of the cross that the sinner can't see Jesus. They want the glory. They would rather be a comet than stars of Bethlehem.

On the Bible

he Bible is the Word of God. Nothing has ever been more clearly established in the world today, and God blesses every people and nation that reverence it. It has stood the test of time. No book has so endured through the ages. No book has been so hated. Everything the cunning of man, philosophy, brutality, could contrive has been done, but it has withstood them all.

There is no book which has such a circulation today. Bibles are dropping from the press like the leaves in autumn. There are 200,000,000 copies. It is read by all nations. It has been translated into five hundred languages and dialects.

No book ever came by luck or chance. Every book owes its existence to some being or beings, and within the range and scope of human intelligence there are but three things—good, bad, and God. All that originates in intellect, all which the intellect can comprehend, must come from one of the three. This book, the Bible, could not possibly be the product of evil, wicked, godless, corrupt, vile men, for it pronounces the heaviest penalties against sin. Like produces like, and if bad men were writing the Bible they never would have pronounced condemnation and punishment against wrongdoing. The holy men of old, we are told, "spake as they were moved by the Holy Ghost." Men do not attribute these beautiful and matchless and well-arranged sentences to human intelligence alone, but we are told that men spake as they were inspired by the Holy Ghost. The only being left, to whom you or I or any sensible person could ascribe the origin of the Bible, is God.

Men have been thrown to beasts and burned to death for having a Bible in their possession. There have been wars over the Bible; cities have been destroyed. Nothing ever brought such persecution as the Bible. Everything vile, dirty, rotten, and iniquitous has been brought to bear against it because it reveals man's cussedness. But it's here, and its power and influence are greater today than ever.

Saloons, bawdy houses, gambling hells, every rake, every white-slaver, every panderer and everything evil has been against it, but it is the word of God, and millions of people know it.

This being true, it is of the highest importance that you should think of the truths in it. I'll bet my life that there are hundreds of you that haven't read ten pages of the Bible in ten years. Some of you never open it except at a birth, a marriage or a death, and then just to keep your family records straight. That's a disgrace and an insult. I repeat it, it's a disgrace and an insult. Don't blame God if you wind up in hell, after God warned you, because you didn't take time to read it and think about it.

It is the only book that tells us of a God that we can love, a heaven to win, a hell to shun and a Saviour that can save. Why did God give us the Bible? So that we might believe in Christ. No other book tells us this. It tells us why the Bible was written, that we might believe and be saved. You don't read a railroad guide to learn to raise buckwheat. You don't read a cookbook to learn to shoe horses. You don't read an arithmetic to learn the history of the United States. A geography does not tell you about how to make buckwheat cakes. No, you read a rail-road guide to learn about the trains, a cookbook to learn to make buckwheat cakes, an arithmetic for arithmetic and a geography for geography. If you want to get out of a book what the author put in it, find out why it was written. That's the way to get good out of a book. Read it.

The Bible was written that you might read and believe that Jesus is the Son of God. The Bible wasn't intended for a history or a cook-book. It was intended to keep me from going to hell.

The greatest good can be had from anything by using it for the purpose for which it was intended. A loaf of bread and a brick may look alike, but try and exchange them and see. You build a house with brick, but you can't eat it. The purpose of a time-table is to give the time of trains, the junctions, the different railroads. A man that has been over the road knows more about it than a man who has never been over it. A man who has made the journey of life guided by the Bible knows more about it than any high-browed lobster who has never lived a word of it. Then whom are you going to believe, the man who has tried it or the man who knows nothing about it?

The Bible was not intended for a science any more than a crowbar is intended for a toothpick. The Bible was written to tell men that they might live, and it's true today.

One man says: "I do not believe in the Bible because of its inconsistencies." I say the greatest inconsistency is in your life—not in the Bible! I bring up before you the memory of some evil deed, and you immediately begin to find fault with the Bible! Go to a man and talk business or politics and he talks sense. Go to a woman and talk society, clubs or dress, and she talks sense. Talk religion to them, and they will talk nonsense!

I want to say that I believe that the Bible is the Word of God from cover to cover. Not because I understand its philosophy, speculation, or theory. I cannot; wouldn't attempt it; and I would be a fool if I tried. I believe it because it is from the mouth of God; the mouth of God has spoken it.

There is only one way to have the doubts destroyed. Read the Bible and obey it. You say you can't understand it. There's an A, B, C in religion, just as in everything else. When you go to school you learn the A, B, C's and pretty soon can understand something you thought you never could when you started out. So in religion. Begin with the simple things and go on and you'll understand. That's what it was written for, that you might read and believe and be saved. I'm willing to stand here and take the hand of any man or woman if you are willing to come and begin with the knowledge you have.

In South Africa there are diamond mines and the fact has been heralded to every corner of the world. But only those that dig for them get the diamonds. So it is with the Bible. Dig and you'll find gold and salvation. You have to dig out the truths.

Years ago in Sing Sing prison there was a convict by the name of Jerry McCauley and one day an old pal of his came back to the prison and told him how he had been saved, and quoted a verse of Scripture. McCauley didn't know where to find the verse in the Bible, so he started in at the first and read through until he came to it. It was away over in the ninth chapter of Hebrews. But he found Jesus Christ while he was reading it. He lived a godly life until the day he died.

Supposing a man should come to you and say, "The title to your property is no good and if some one contests it you will lose?" Would you laugh and go on about your business? No, sir! You would go to the courthouse and if you could find it in only one book there, the book in the recorder's office, you'd search and find it, and if the recorder said the deed was all right you could laugh at whatever anyone else said.

There is only one book in the world that tells me about my soul. It says if you believe you're saved, if you don't you are damned. God said it and it's all true. Every man who believes in the Bible shall live forever. The Bible says heaven or hell, so why do you resist?

No words are put in the Bible for effect. The Bible talks to us so we can understand. God could use language that no one could understand. But we cannot understand all by simply hearing and reading. When we see we will know.

> "I stood one day beside a blacksmith's door,
>   And heard the anvil beat and the bellows chime;
> Looking in, I saw upon the floor
>   Old hammers worn out with beating years and years of time.
>
> " 'How many anvils have you had?' said I,
>   'To wear and batter all these hammers so?'
> 'Just one,' said he, then said with twinkling eye,
>   'The anvil wears the hammers out, you know.'
>
> "So methought, the anvils of God's word—
>   Of Jesus' sacrifice—have been beat upon—
> The noise of falling blows was heard—
>   The anvil is unharmed—the hammers are all gone."

Julian the apostate was a hammer. Gone! Voltaire, Renan, hammers. Gone! In Germany, Goethe, Strauss, Schleiermacher—gone. In England, Mill, Hume, Hobbes, Darwin, Huxley, and Spencer—the anvil remains; the hammer is gone. In America, Thomas Paine, Parker, Ingersoll, gone. The anvil remains.

Listen. In France a hundred years ago or more they were printing and circulating infidel literature at the expense of $4,500,000 a year. What was the result? God was denied, the Bible sneered at and ridiculed, and between 1792 and 1795 one million twenty thousand and fifty-one hundred people were brought to death. The Word of God stood unshaken amidst it all. Josh Billings said: "I would rather be an idiot than an infidel; because if I am an infidel I made myself so, but if I am an idiot somebody else did it." Oh, the wreckers' lights on the dangerous coasts that try to allure and drag us away from God have all gone out, but God's words shine on.

The vital truths of the Bible are more believed in the world today than at any other time. When a man becomes so intelligent that he cannot accept the Bible, too progressive to be a Christian, that man's influence for good, in society, in business or as a companion, is at an end. Some think that being a doubter is an evidence of superior intellect. No!

I've never found a dozen men in my life who disbelieved in the Bible but what they were hugging some secret sin. When you are willing to give up that pet sin you will find it easy to believe in the Bible.

It explains to me why Saul of Tarsus, the murderer, was changed to Paul, the apostle. It explains to me why David Livingstone left his Highland home to go to darkest Africa. It explains to me why the Earl of Shaftesbury was made from a drunkard into a power for God in London for sixty-five years. It explains why missionaries leave home and friends to go into unknown lands and preach Jesus Christ, and perhaps to die at the hands of the natives.

I can see in this book God revealed to man and when I do and accept, I am satisfied. It is just what you need to be satisfied. God knows your every need.

This explains to me why Jesus Christ has such influence on men and women in the world today. No man ever had such influence to teach men and women virtue and goodness as Christ. This influence has been in the world from 2,000 years ago to the present time. The human heart is to Jesus like a great piano. First he plays the sad melodies of repentance and then the joyful hallelujahs.

The Bible has promises running all through it and God wants you to appropriate them for your use. They are like a bank note. They are of no value unless used. You might starve to death if you have money in your pockets, but won't use it. So the promises may not do you any good because you will not use them. The Bible is a galaxy of promises like the Milky Way in the heavens.

When you are in trouble, instead of going to your Bible, you let them grow, and they grow faster than Jonah's gourd vine. You're afraid to step out on the promises.

There are many exceedingly great and precious promises in the Bible. Here is one:

"Whatsoever ye shall ask in my name, that will I do, that the Father may be glorified in the Son."

If some of you would receive such a promise from John D. Rockefeller or Andrew Carnegie, you'd sit up all night writing out checks to be cashed in the morning. And yet you let the Bible lie on the table.

But the infidel says: "Mr. Sunday, why are there so many intelligent people in the world that don't believe the Bible?"

Do you wonder that it was an infidel woman, that first started the question: "Is marriage a failure?" A fool, infidel woman. Christians do not ask such fool questions. Would you be surprised to be reminded that infidel writers and speakers have always and do always advocate and condone and excuse suicide? Do you know that in infidelity the Gospel is suicide? That is their theory and I don't blame them, and the sooner they leave the world the better the world will be.

The great men of the ages are on the side of the Bible. A good many infidels talk as though the great minds of the world were arrayed against Christianity and the Bible. Great statesmen, investors, painters, poets, artists, musicians, have lifted up their hearts in prayer. Watt, the inventor of the steam engine, was a Christian; Fulton, the inventor of the steamboat, was a Christian; Cyrus McCormick, who first invented the self-binder, was a Christian; Morse, who invented the telegraph, and the first message that ever flashed over the wire was from Deuteronomy—"What hath God wrought." Edison, although a doubter in some things, said that there was evidence enough in chemistry to prove the existence of a God, if there was no evidence besides that. George Washington was a Christian. Abraham Lincoln was a Christian, and with Bishop Simpson knelt on his knees in the White House, praying God to give victory to the Army of the Blue. John Hay, the brightest

Secretary of State that ever managed the affairs of state, in my judgment, was a Christian, William Jennings Bryan, a man as clean as a hound's tooth; Garfield, McKinley, Grover Cleveland, Harrison, Theodore Roosevelt, Woodrow Wilson—all Christians.

The poets drew their inspiration from the Bible. Dante's "Inferno," Milton's "Paradise Lost," two of the greatest works ever written, were inspired by the Word of God. Lord Byron, although a profligate, drew his inspiration from the Word of God. Shakespeare's works abound with quotations from the Bible. John G. Whittier, Longfellow, Michelangelo, who painted "The Last Judgment," Raphael, who painted the "Madonna of the Chair," DaVinci, who painted "The Last Supper," all dipped their brushes in the light of heaven and painted for eternity. The great men of the world of all ages, of science, art, or statesmanship, have all believed in Jesus Christ as the Son of God.

Years ago, with the Holy Spirit for my guide, I entered this wonderful temple that we call Christianity. I entered through the portico of Genesis and walked down through the Old Testament's art gallery, where I saw the portraits of Joseph, Jacob, Daniel, Moses, Isaiah, Solomon and David hanging on the wall; I entered the music room of the Psalms and the Spirit of God struck the keyboard of my nature until it seemed to me that every reed and pipe in God's great organ of nature responded to the harp of David, and the charm of King Solomon in his moods.

I walked into the business house of Proverbs.

I walked into the observatory of the prophets and there saw photographs of various sizes, some pointing to far-off stars or events—all concentrated upon one great Star which was to rise as an atonement for sin.

Then I went into the audience room of the King of Kings, and got a vision from four different points—from Matthew, Mark, Luke and John. I went into the correspondence room, and saw Peter, James, Paul and Jude, penning their epistles to the world. I went into the Acts of the Apostles and saw the Holy Spirit forming the Holy Church, and then I walked into the throne room and saw a door at the foot of a tower and, going up, I saw One standing there, fair as the morning, Jesus Christ, the Son of God, and I found this truest friend that man ever knew; when all were false I found him true.

In teaching me the way of life, the Bible has taught me the way to live, it taught me how to die.

So that is why I am here, sober and a Christian, instead of a booze-hoisting infidel.

Teach Us to Pray

We live and develop physically by exercise. We are saved by faith, but we must work out our salvation by doing the things God wills. The more we do for God, the more God will do through us. Faith will increase by experience.

If you are a stranger to prayer you are a stranger to the greatest source of power known to human beings. If we cared for our physical life in the same lackadaisical way that we care for our spiritual, we would be as weak physically as we are spiritually. You go week in and week out without prayer. I want to be a giant for God. You don't ever sing; you let the choir do it. You go to prayer-meeting and offer no testimony.

You are a stranger to the great privilege that is offered to human beings. Some of the greatest blessings that people enjoy come from prayer. In earnest prayer you think as the Lord directs, and lose yourself in him.

Some people say, "It's no use to pray. The Lord knows everything, anyway." That's true. He does. He is not limited. He knows everything and has known it since before the world was. We don't know everybody who is going to be converted at this revival, but that doesn't relieve us of our duty. We don't know, and we must do the work he has commanded us to do.

Others say: "But I don't get what I pray for." Well, there's a cause for everything. Get at the cause and you'll be all right. If you are sick and send for the doctor, he pays no attention to the disease, but looks at what produced it. If you have a headache, don't rub your forehead. In Matthew it is written, "Ask and it shall be given you; seek and ye shall find; knock and it shall be opened unto you." If your prayers are not answered you are not right with God. If you have no faith, if your motive is wrong, then your prayers will be in vain. Many times when people pray they are selfish. They are not gripping the word. I believe that when a wife prays for the conversion of her husband it isn't because she really desires the salvation of his soul, but because she thinks if he were converted things would be easier for her personally. Pray for your neighbors as well as your own family. The pastor of one church does not pray for the congregation of another denomination. I'm not saying anything against denominations, I believe in them. I believe they are of God. Denominations represent different temperaments. A man with warm emotions would not make a good Episcopalian, but he would make a crackerjack Methodist. Oh, the curse of selfishness! The Church is dying for religion, for religion pure and undefiled. Pure religion and undefiled is visiting the widow and the father and doing the will of God without so much thought of yourself. I tell you, a lot of people are going to be fooled the Day of Judgement.

Isaiah says the hand of God is not shortened and his ear is not deaf. No, his hand is not shortened so that it cannot save. He has provided agencies by which we can be saved. If he had made no provision for your salvation, then the trouble would be with God; but he has, so if you go to hell the trouble will be with you.

In Ezekiel we read that men have taken idols into their hearts and put stumbling-blocks before their faces. God is not going to hear you if you place clothes, money, pride of relationship before him. You know there is sin in your life. Many people know there is sin in their lives, yet ask God to bless them. They ought first to get down on their knees and pray, "God be merciful to me a sinner."

Some people are too contemptibly stingy for God to hear them. God won't hear you if you stop your ears to the cries of the poor. You drag along here for three weeks and raise a paltry sum that a circus would take out of town in two hours. When they give things to the poor they rip off the buttons and the fine braid. Some people pick out old clothes that the moths have made into sieves and give them to the poor and think they are charitable. That isn't charity, no sir; it's charity when you'll give something you'll miss. It's charity when you feel it to give.

And when you stand praying, forgive if you have aught against anyone. It's no use to pray if you have a mean, miserable disposition, if you are grouchy, if you quarrel in your home or with your neighbors.

It's no use to pray for a blessing when you have a fuss on with your neighbors. It doesn't do any good. You go to a sewing society meeting to make mosquito neeting for the Eskimo and blankets for the Hottentots, and instead you sit and chew the rag and rip some women up the back. The spirit of God flees from strife and discord.

People say: "She is a good woman, but a worldly Christian." What? Might as well speak of a heavenly devil. Might as well expect a mummy to speak and bear children as that kind to move the world Godward. Prayer draws you nearer to God.

"Teach us to pray," implies that I want to be taught. It's a great privilege to be taught by Jesus. A friend of mine was preaching out in Cedar Rapids, Iowa, and had to go to a hospital in Chicago for an operation, and I was asked to go and preach in his place. Alexander was leading the singing, and one night Charles called a little girl out of the audience to sing. She didn't look over four or five years of age, though she might have been a little older. I thought, "What's the use? Her little voice can never be heard over this crowd." But Charlie stood her up in a chair by the pulpit and she threw back her head and out rolled some of the sweetest music I have ever heard. It was wonderful. I sat there and the tears streamed down my checks. That little girl was the daughter of a Northwestern engineer and he took her to Chicago when her mother was away. Some one took her to Patti. Patti took the little girl to one of her suite of rooms and told her to stand there and sing. Then she went to the other end of the suite and sat down on a divan and listened. The song moved her to tears. She ran and hugged and kissed the little girl and sat her down on the divan and said to her; "Now you sit here and I'll go over there and sing." She took up her position where the child had stood, and she lifted her magnificent voice and she sang "Home, Sweet Home" and "The Last Rose of Summer"—sang them for that little girl! And Patti used to get a thousand dollars for a song, too. She always knew how many songs she was to sing, for she had a check before she went on the platform. It was a great privilege the little daughter of that Northwestern engineer had, but it's a greater privilege to learn from Jesus Christ how to pray.

A friend of mine told me he went to hear Paganini, and the great violinist broke one of the strings on his instrument, then another, then another, until he had only one left, and on that one he played so wonderfully that his audience burst into terrific applause. It was a privilege to hear that, but it's a greater privilege to have Jesus teach you how to pray.

Let us take a few examples from the life of Christ. In Mark we learn that he rose up early in the morning and went out to a solitary place and prayed. He began every day with prayer. You never get up without dressing. You forget to wash your face and comb your hair. You always think of breakfast. You feed your physical body. Why do you starve your spiritual body? If nine-tenths of you were as weak physically as you are spiritually, you couldn't walk.

When I was assistant secretary of the Y.M.C.A. at Chicago, John G. Paton came home from the New Hebrides and was lecturing and collecting money. He was raising money to buy a sea-going steam yatch, for his work took him from island to island and he had to use a rowboat, and sometimes it was dangerous when the weather was bad, so he wanted the yacht. We had him a week, and it was my privilege to go to lunch with him. We would go out to a restaurant at noon and he would talk to us. Sometimes there would be as many as fifteen or twenty preachers in the crowd, and now and then some of us were so interested in what he told us of the work for Jesus in those far-away islands that we forgot to eat. I remember that he said one day: "All that I am I owe to my Christian father and mother. My father was one of the most prayful men I ever knew. Often in the daytime he would slip into his closet, and he would drop a handkerchief outside the door, and when we children saw the white sentinel we knew that father was talking with God and would go quietly away. It is largely because of the life and influence of that same saintly father that I am preaching to the cannibals in the South Seas." It is an insult to God and a disgrace to allow children to grow up without throwing Christian influences around them. Seven-tenths of professing Christians have no family prayers and do not read the Bible. It is no wonder the damnable ballrooms are wrecking the virtue of our girls.

In the fourteenth chapter of Matthew it is told that when Jesus had sent the multitudes away he went up into the mountain and was there alone with God. Jesus Christ never forgot to thank God for answering his prayers. Jesus asked him to help feed the multitude, and he didn't neglect to thank him for it. Next time you pray don't ask God for anything. Just try to think of all the things you have to be thankful for, and tell him about them.

Pride keeps us from prayer. Being chesty and big-headed is responsible for more failures than anything else in this world. It has spoiled many an employee. Some fellows get a job and in about two weeks they think they know more about the business than the boss does. They think he is all wrong. It never occurs to them that it took some brains and some knowledge to build that business up and keep it running till they got there.

Here's two things to guard against. Don't get chesty over success, or discouraged over a seeming defeat.

"And when he prayed he said: 'Lazarus, come forth'; and he that was dead came forth." If we prayed right we would raise men from sin and bring them forth into the light of righteousness.

"And as he prayed the fashion of his countenance was alerted." Ladies, do you want to look pretty? If some of you women would spend less on dope and cold cream and get down on your knees and pray, God would make you prettier. Why, I can look into your faces and tell what sort of lives you live. If you are devoting your time and thoughts to society, your countenance will show it. If you pray, I can see that.

Every man who has helped to light up the dark places of the world has been a praying man. I never preach a sermon until I've soaked it in prayer. Never. Then I never forget to thank God for helping me when I preach. I don't care whether you read your prayers out of a book or whether you just say them, so long as you mean them. A man can read his prayers and go to heaven, or he may just say his prayers and go to hell. We've got to face conditions. When I read I find that all the saintly men who have done things from Pentecost until today, have known how to pray. It was a master stroke of the devil when he got the church to give up prayer. One of the biggest farces today is the average prayer-meeting.

Matthew says, "But thou, when thou prayest, enter into the closet, and when thou hast shut the door, pray to thy Father, which is in secret; and thy Father which seeth in secret shall reward thee openly."

Two men came to the Temple to pray—the first was the Pharisee. He was nice and smooth, and his attitude was nice and smooth. He prayed: "God, I thank thee that I am not as other men are, extortioners, unjust, adulterers, or even as this publican. I fast twice in the week, I give tithes of all I possess," and he went out. I can imagine a lot of people sitting around the church and saying: "That is my idea of religion; that is it. I am no sensationalist; I don't want anything vulgar, no slang." Why don't you use a little, bud, so that something will come your way? And it will come as straight as two and two make four.

Services rendered in such opposite directions cannot meet with the same results. If two men were on the top of a tall building and one should jump and one come down the fire escape they couldn't expect to meet with the same degree of safety. The Pharisee said, "Thank God, I am not as other men are," and the publican said, "God be merciful to me, a sinner." The first man went to his house the same as when he came out of it. "God be merciful to me, a sinner." That man was justified. I am justified in my faith in Jesus Christ. I am no longer a sinner. I am justified as though I had never sinned by faith in the Son of God. That man went down to his home justified.

How many people pray in a real sense? How many people pray in humility and truth? Some men pray for humility when it is pride they want. Many a man gets down on his knees and says: "Our Father, who art in heaven, hallowed be thy name: thy kingdom come . . ." That is not so; they don't want God's kingdom to come. It is not so with half the people that pray. I say to you when you pray in the church pew and say that, it don't count a snap of my finger if you don't live it. You pray, "Thy kingdom come," and then you go out and do something to prevent that kingdom from coming. No man can get down and pray "Thy kingdom come," and have a beer wagon back up to his door and put beer in the ice box. No man can get down on his knees and pray "Thy Kingdom come," and look through the bottom of a beer glass. God won't stand for it. If you wanted God's will done you would do God's will, even if it took every drop of blood in your body to do it.

"Thy will be done on earth as it is in heaven." When you say this in your pew on Sunday it means nothing unless you live it on Monday. You say "Thy kingdom come," and then go out and do the very thing that will prevent God's kingdom from coming. Your prayers or anything you do in the church on Sunday mean nothing if you don't do the same thing in business on Monday. I don't care how loud your wind-jamming in prayer-meeting may be if you go out and skin somebody in a horse deal the next day.

The man who truly prays, "Thy kingdom come," cannot take his heart out of his prayer when he is out of the church. The man who truly prays "Thy kingdom come," will not be shrinking his measures at the store; the load of coal he sends to you won't be half slate. The man who truly prays "Thy kingdom come" won't cut off his yard-stick when he measures you a piece of calico. It will not take the pure-food law to keep a man who truly prays "Thy kingdom come" from putting chalk in the flour, sand in the sugar, brick dust in red pepper, ground peanut shell in breakfast food.

The man who truly prays "Thy kingdom come" cannot pass a saloon and not ask himself the question, "What can I do to get rid of that thing that is blighting the lives of thousands of young men, that is wrecking homes, and that is dragging men and women down to hell?" You cannot pray "Thy kingdom come," and then rush to the polls and vote for the thing that is preventing that kingdom from coming. You cannot pray "Thy kingdom come" and then go do the things that make the devil laugh. For the man who truly prays "Thy kingdom come" it would be impossible to have one kind of religion in the pew and another in politics. When a man truly prays "Thy kingdom come" he means it in everything or in nothing.

A lot of church members are praying wrong. You should pray first, "God be merciful to me a sinner," and then "Thy kingdom come."

Saying a prayer is one thing: doing God's will is another. Both should be synonymous. Angels are angels because they do God's will. When they refuse to do God's will they become devils.

Many a man prays when he gets in a hole. Many a man prays when he is up against it. Many a man prays in the time of trouble, but when he can stick his thumbs in his armholes and take a pair of scissors and cut his coupons off, then it is "Good-bye, God; I'll see you later." Many a man will make promises to God in his extremity, but forget them in his prosperity. Many a man will make promises to God when the hearse is backed up to the door to carry the baby out, but will soon forget the promises made in the days of adversity. Many a man will make promises when lying on his back, thinking he is going to die, and load up just the same when he is on his feet.

Every man and every woman that God has used to halt this sin-cursed world and set it going Godward has been a Christian of prayer. Martin Luther arose from his bed and prayed all night, and when the break of day came he called his wife and said to her, "It has come." History records that on that very day King Charles granted religious toleration, a thing for which Luther had prayed.

John Knox, whom his queen feared more than any other man, was in such agony of prayer that he ran out into the street and fell on his face and cried, "O God, give me Scotland or I'll die." And God gave him Scotland and not only that, he threw England in for some measure.

When Jonathan Edwards was about to preach his greatest sermon on "Sinners in the Hands of an Angry God," he prayed for days; and when he stood before the congregation and preached it, men caught at the seats in their terror, and some fell to the floor; and the people cried out in their fear, "Mr. Edwards, tell us how we can be saved!"

The critical period of American history was between 1784 and 1789. There was no common coinage, no common defense. When the colonies sent men to a constitutional convention, Benjamin Franklin, rising with the weight of his four score years, asked that the convention open with prayer, and George Washington there sealed the bargain with God. In that winter in Valley Forge, Washington led his men in prayer and he got down on his knees to do it.

When the battle of Gettysburg was on, Lincoln, old Abe Lincoln, was on his knees with God; yes, he was on his knees from five o'clock in the afternoon till four o'clock in the morning, and Bishop Simpson was with him.

"And whatsoever ye shall ask thy Father in My Name, that will I do, that the Father may be glorified in the Son."

No man can ever be saved without Jesus Christ. There's no way to God unless you come through Jesus Christ. It's Jesus Christ or nothing.

"Lord, teach us to pray."

The Need of Revivals

omebody asks: "What is a revival?" Revival is a purely philosophical, common-sense result of the wise use of divinely appointed means, just the same as water will put out a fire; the same as food will appease your hunger; just the same as water will slake your thirst; it is a philosophical common-sense use of divinely appointed means to accomplish that end. A revival is just as much horse sense as that.

A revival is not material; it does not depend upon material means. It is a false idea that there is something peculiar in it, that it cannot be judged by ordinary rules, causes and effects. That is nonsense. Above your head there is an electric light; that is effect. What is the cause? Why, the dynamo. Religion can be judged on the same basis of cause and effect. If you do a thing, results always come. The results come to the farmer. He has his crops. That is the result. He has to plow and plant and take care of his farm before the crops come.

Religion needs a baptism of horse sense. That is just pure horse sense. I believe there is no doctrine more dangerous to the Church today than to convey the impression that a revival is something peculiar in itself and cannot be judged by the same rules of causes and effect as other things. If you preach that to the farmers—if you go to a farmer and say "God is a sovereign," that is true; if you say "God will give you crops only when it pleases him and it is no use for you to plow your ground and plant your crops in the spring," that is all wrong, and if you preach that doctrine and expect the farmers to believe it, this country will starve to death in two years. The churches have been preaching some false doctrines and religion has died out.

Some people think that religion is a good deal like a storm. They sit around and fold their arms, and that is what is the matter. You sit in your pews so easy that you become mildewed. Such results will be sure to follow if you are persuaded that religion is something mysterious and has not natural connection between the means and the end. It has a natural connection of common sense and I believe that when divinely appointed means are used spiritual blessing will accrue to the individuals and the community in greater numbers than temporal blessings. You can have spiritual blessings as regularly as the farmer can have corn, wheat, oats, or you can have potatoes and onions and cabbage in your garden. I believe that spiritual results will follow more surely than temporal blessings. I don't believe all this tommy-rot of false doctrines. You might as well sit around beneath the shade and fan yourself and say "Ain't it hot?" as to expect God to give you a crop if you don't plow the ground and plant the seed. Until the Church resorts to the use of divinely appointed means it won't get the blessing.

What is a revival? Now listen to me. A revival does two things. First, it returns the Church from her backsliding and second, it causes the conversion of men and women; and it always includes the conviction of sin on the part of the Church. What a spell the devil seems to cast over the Church today!

I suppose the people here are pretty fair representatives of the Church of God, and if everybody did what you do there were would never be a revival. Suppose I did no more than you do, then no people would ever be converted through my efforts; I would fold my arms and rust out. A revival helps to bring the unsaved to Jesus Christ.

God Almighty never intended that the devil should triumph over the Church. He never intended that the saloons should walk rough-shod over Christianity. And if you think that anybody is going to frighten me, you don't know me yet.

When is a revival needed? When the individuals are careless and un-concerned. If the Church were down on her face in prayer they would be more concerned with the fellow outside. The Church has degenerated into a third-rate amusement joint, with religion left out.

When is a revival needed? When carelessness and unconcern keep the people asleep. It is as much the duty of the Church to awaken and work and labor for the men and women of this city as it is the duty of the fire department to rush out when the call sounds. What would you think of the fire department if it slept while the town burned? You would condemn them, and I will condemn you if you sleep and let men and women go to hell. It is just as much your business to be wake. The Church of God is asleep today; it is turned into a dormitory, and has taken the devil's opiates.

When may a revival be expected? When the wickedness of the wicked grieves and distresses the Christian. Sometimes people don't seem to mind the sins of other people. Don't seem to mind while boys and girls walk the streets of their city and know more of evil than gray-haired men. You are asleep.

When is a revival needed? When the Christians have lost the spirit of prayer.

When is a revival needed? When you feel the want of revival and feel the need of it. Men have had this feeling, ministers have had it until they thought they would die unless a revival would come to awaken their people, their students, their deacons and their Sunday-school workers, unless they would fall down on their faces and renounce the world and the works and deceits of the devil. When the Church of God draws its patrons from the theaters the theaters will close up, or else take the dirty, rotten plays off the stage.

When the Church of God stops voting for the saloon, the saloon will go to hell. When the members stop having cards in their homes, there won't be so many black-legged gamblers in the world. This is the truth. You can't sit around and fold your arms and let God run this business; you have been doing that too long here. When may a revival be expected? When Christians confess their sins one to another. Sometimes they confess in a general way, but they have no earnestness; they get up and do it in eloquent language, but that doesn't do it. It is when they break down and cry and pour out their hearts to God in grief, when the flood-gates open, then I want to tell you the devil will have cold feet.

When may a revival be expected? When the wickedness of the wicked grieves and distresses the Church. When you are willing to make a sacrifice for the revival; when you are willing to sacrifice your feelings. You say, "Oh, well, Mr. Sunday hurt my feelings." Then don't spread them all over his tabernacle for men to walk on. I despise a touchy man or woman. Make a sacrifice of your feelings; make a sacrifice of your business, of your time, of your money; you are willing to give to help to advance God's cause, for God's cause has to have money the same as a railroad or a steamship company. When you give your influence and stand up and let people know you stand for Jesus Christ and it has your indorsement and time and money. Somebody has got to get on the firing line. Somebody had to go on the firing line and become bullet meat for $13 a month to overcome slavery. Somebody has to be willing to make a sacrifice. They must be willing to get out and hustle and do things for God.

When may a revival be expected? A revival may be expected when Christian people confess and ask forgiveness for their sins. When you are willing that God shall promote and use whatever means or instruments or individuals or methods he is pleased to use to promote them. Yes. The trouble is he cannot promote a revival if you are sitting on the judgment of the methods and means that God is employing to promote a revival. The God Almighty may use any method or means or individual that he pleases in order to promote a revival. You are not running it. Let God have his way. You can tell whether you need a revival. You can tell if you will have one and why you have got one. If God should ask you sisters and preachers in an audible voice, "Are you willing that I should promote a revival by using any methods or means or individual language that I choose to use to promote it?" what would be your answer? Yes. Then don't growl if I use some things that you don't like. You have no business to. How can you promote a revival? Break up your fallow ground, the ground that produces nothing but weeds, briars, tin cans and brick-bats. Fallow ground is ground that never had a glow in it. Detroit had a mayor, Pingree, when Detroit had thousands and thousands of acres of fallow ground. This was taken over by the municipal government and planted with potatoes with which they fed the poor of the city.

There are individuals who have never done anything for Jesus Christ, and I have no doubt there are preachers as well, who have never done anything for the God Almighty. There are acres and acres of fallow ground lying right here that have never been touched. Look over your past life, look over your present life and future and take up the individual sins and with pencil and paper write them down. A general confession will never do. You have committed your sins, one by one, and you will have to confess them one by one. This thing of saying, "God, I am a sinner," won't do.

"God, I am a gossiper in my neighborhood. God, I have been in my ice-box while I am here listening to Mr. Sunday." Confess your sins.

How can you promote a revival? You women, if you found that your husband was giving his love and attention to some other woman and if you saw that some other woman was encroaching on his mind and heart, and was usurping your place and was pushing you out of the place, wouldn't you grieve? Don't you think that God grieves when you push him out of your life? You don't treat God square. You business-men don't treat God fair. You let a thousand things come in and take the place that God Almighty had. No wonder you are careless. You blame God for things you have no right to blame him for. He is not to blame for anything. You judge God. The spirit loves the Bible; the devil loves the flesh.

If you don't do your part, don't blame God. How many times have you blamed God when you are the liar yourself. You are wont to blame him for the instances of unbelief that have come into your life. When should be promote a revival? When there is a neglect of prayer? When your prayers affect God? You never think of going out on the street without dressing. You would be pinched before you went a block. You never think of going without breakfast, do you? I bet there are multi-tudes that have come here without reading the Bible or praying for this meeting.

You can measure your desire for salvation by means of the amount of self-denial you are willing to practice for Jesus Christ. You have sinned before the Church, before the world, before God.

Don't the Lord have a hard time? Own up, now.

There are a lot of people in church, doubtless, who have denied them-selves—self-denial for comfort and convenience. There are a lot of peo-ple here who never make any sacrifices for Jesus Christ. They will not suffer any reproaches for Jesus Christ. Paul says, "I love to suffer re-proaches for Christ." The Bible says, "Woe unto you when all men shall speak well of you." "Blessed are you when your enemies persecute you." That is one trouble in the churches of God today. They are not willing to suffer reproach for God's sake. It would be a godsend if the Church would suffer persecution today; she hasn't suffered it for hun-dreds of years. She is growing rich and lagging behind. Going back.

Pride! How many times have you found yourself exercising pride?

How many times have you attempted pride of wealth? Proud because you were related to some of the old families that settled in the Colonies in 1776. That don't get you anything; not at all. I have got as much to be proud of as to lineage as anyone; my great-grandfather was in the Revolutionary War, lost a leg at Brandywine; and my father was a soldier in the Civil War.

Envy! Envy of those that have more talent than you. Envious because someone can own a limousine Packard and you have to ride a Brush runabout; envious because some women can wear a sealskin coat and you a nearseal.

Then there is your grumbling and fault-finding. When speaking of people behind their backs, telling their fault, whether real or imaginary, and that is slander. When you sit around and rip people up behind their backs at your old sewing societies, when you rip and tear and discuss your neighbors and turn the affair into a sort of a great big gossiping society, with your fault-finding, grumbling and growling. There is a big difference between levity and happiness, and pleasure, and all that sort of thing.

Make up your mind that God has given himself up for you. I would like to see something come thundering along that I would have more interest in than I have in the cause of God Almighty! God has a right to the first place. God is first, remember that.

Multitudes of people are willing to do anything that doesn't require any self-denial on their part.

I am not a member of any lodge, and never expect to be, but if I were a member of a lodge, and there were a prayer-meeting and a lodge-meeting coming on Wednesday night, I would be at the prayer-meeting instead of at the lodge-meeting. I am not against the lodges; they do some good work in the world, but that doesn't save anyone for God. God is first and the lodge-meeting is second. God is first and society second. God is first and business is second. "In the beginning, God!" That is the way the Bible starts out and it ought to be the way with every living being. "In the beginning, God." Seek you first God and everything else shall be added unto you. Christianity is addition; sin is subtraction. Christianity is peace, joy, salvation, heaven. Sin takes away peace, happiness, sobriety, and it takes away health. You are robbing God of the time that you misspend. You are robbing God when you spend time doing something that don't amount to anything, when you might do something for Christ. You are robbing God when you go to foolish amusements, when you sit around reading trashy novels instead of the Word of God.

"Oh, Lord, revive thy work!"

I have only two minutes more and then I am through. Bad temper. Abuse your wife and abuse your children; abuse your husband; turn your old gatling-gun tongue loose. A lady came to me and said, "Mr. Sunday, I know I have a bad temper, but I am over with it in a minute." So is the shotgun, but it blows everything to pieces.

And, finally, you abuse the telephone girl because she doesn't connect you in a minute. Bad temper. I say you abuse your wife, you go cussing around if supper isn't ready on time; cussing because the coffee isn't hot; you dig your fork into a hunk of beefsteak and put it on your plate and then you say: "Where did you get this, in the harness shop? Take it out and make a hinge for the door."Then you go to your store, or office, and smile and everybody thinks you are an angel about to sprout wings and fly to the imperial realm above. Bad temper! You growl at your children; you snap and snarl around the house until they have to go to the neighbors to see a smile. They never get a kind word —no wonder so many of them go to the devil quick.

Consecration

beseech you, therefore, brethren, by the mercies of God, that ye present your bodies a living sacrifice, holy, acceptable until God, which is your reasonable service."

The armies of God are never made up of drafted men and women, ordered into service whether willing or not. God never owned a slave. God doesn't want you to do anything that you can't do without protest. This is not a call to hard duty, but an invitation to the enjoyment of a privelege. It is not a call to hired labor to take the hoe and go into the field, but the appeal of a loving father to his children to partake of all he has to give.

If there is nothing in you that will respond to God's appeal when you think of his mercies, I don't think much of you. The impelling motive of my text is gratitude, not fear. It looks to Calvary, not to Sinai. We are being entreated, not threatened. That's the amazing thing to me. To think that God would entreat us—would stand to entreat us! He is giving me a chance to show I love him.

If you are not ready to offer it in gratitude, God doesn't want you to serve him through fear, but because you realize his love for you, and appreciate and respond to it.

A business man who loves his wife will never be too busy to do something for her, never too busy to stop sometimes to think of how good she has been and what she has done for him. If men would only think of the things God has done for them there would be less card-playing, less thought of dinners and of concerts and other diversions of the world. God wants us to sit down and think over his goodness to us. The man who doesn't isn't worth a nickel a punch. Has God done anything for us as a nation, has he done anything for us as individuals, that commands our gratitude?

Astronomers have counted three hundred and eighty million stars, and they have barely commenced. Why, you might as well try to count those countless stars as to try to count God's mercies. You might as well try to count the drops of water in the sea or the grains of sand upon the shore. If we only think, we shall say with David: "According to Thy tender mercies."

An old lady said one morning that she would try to count all God's mercies for that one day, but at noon she was becoming confused, and at three o'clock she threw up her hands and said: "They come three times too fast for me to count."

Just think of the things we have to be thankful for! A visitor to an insane asylum was walking through the grounds and as he passed one of the buildings he heard a voice from a barred window high up in the wall and it said: "Stranger, did you ever thank God for your reason?" He had never thought of that before, but he says that he has thought of it every day since. Did you ever think that thousands of people who were just as good as you are, are beating their heads against the walls of padded cells? Did you ever think what a blessed thing it is that you are sane and you go about among men and follow your daily duties, and go home to be greeted by your wife and have your children climb about you?

Did you ever thank God for your eyes? Did you ever thank him that you can see the sunrise and the sunset and can see the flowers and the trees and look upon the storm? Did you ever thank God that you have two good eyes while so many others less fortunate than you must grope their way in blindness to the coffin?

Did you ever thank God for hearing? That you can hear music and the voices of friends and dear ones? That you can leave your home and business, and come here and hear the songs and the preaching of the word of God? Did you ever think what it would mean to be deaf?

Did you ever thank God for the blessing of taste? Some people can't tell whether they are eating sawdust and shavings or strawberries and ice cream. Think of the good things we enjoy! Others have tastes so vicious that they find it almost impossible to eat. God might have made our food taste like quinine.

Did you ever thank God that you can sleep? If not, you ought to be kept awake for a month. Think of the thousands who suffer from pain or insomnia so that they can sleep only under opiates. Did you ever wake up on the morning and thank God that you have had a good night's rest? If you haven't, God ought to keep you awake for a week, then you'd know you've had reason to be thankful.

Did you ever thank God for the doctors and nurses and hospitals? For the surgeon who comes with scalpel to save your life or relieve your sufferings? If it had not been for them, you'd be under the grass. For the nurse who watches over you that you may be restored to health?

Did you ever thank God for the bread you eat, while so many others are hungry? Did you ever thank him for the enemy that has been baffled for the lie against you that has failed?

Out in Elgin, Illinois, I was taken driving by a friend, and he said that he wanted me to go with him to see a man. He took me to see a man who was lying in bed, with arms most pitifully wasted by suffering. The poor fellow said he had been in bed for thirty-two years, but he wasn't worrying about that. He said he was so sorry for the well people who didn't know Jesus. I went out thanking God that I could walk. If your hearts are not made of stone or adamant they will melt with gratitude when you think of the many mercies, the tender mercies, of God.

"Brethren"—that's what God calls his true followers. No speaking from the loft. If there's any lesson we need to learn it is that of being "brethren."

Sinners are not called "brethren" in the Bible. God commands sinners. They are in rebellion. He entreats Christians. When Lincoln called for volunteers, he addressed men as "citizens of the United States," not as foreigners.

The man who is appreciative of God's mercies will not have much mercy on himself. Don't stand up and say: "I'll do what Jesus bids me to do, and go where he bids me to go," then go to bed. Present your bodies—not mine—not those of your wives; you must present your own. Present your bodies; not your neighbor's; not your children's; it is their duty to do that. Do you trust God enough to let him do what he wants to do?

Henry Varley said to Moody, when that great American was in England, that God is waiting to show this world what one man could do for him. Moody said: "Varley, by the grace of God I'll be that man"; and God took hold of Moody and shook the world with him. God would shake the world with us today if only we would present our bodies as a living sacrifice to him, as Moody did. Are you willing to present yourself? I am tired of a church of five hundred of seven hundred members without power enough to bring one soul to Christ.

At the opening of the Civil War many a man was willing that the country should be saved by able-bodied male relatives of his wife, who made themselves bullet-men, but he didn't go himself. God isn't asking for other men's bodies. He's asking for yours. If you would all give to God what rightfully belongs to him, I tell you he would create a commotion on earth and in hell. If God had the feet of some of you he would point your toes in different ways from those you have been going for many years. If he had your feet he would never head you into a booze joint. If he had your feet he would never send you into a ballroom. If he had the feet of some of you he would make you wear out shoe leather lugging back what you've taken that doesn't belong to you. If God had your feet he would take you to prayer meeting. I'm afraid the preacher would have nervous prostration, for he hasn't seen some of you there in years. If God had your feet, you'd find it harder to follow the devil. Some of you preachers have you children going to dancing school and I hear some of you go to dances. He would make your daily walk conform to the Golden Rule and the Sermon on the Mount.

Some people work only with their mouths. God wants that part that's on the ground. Some soldiers sit around and smell the coffee and watch the bacon frying.

If God had your hands, he would make you let go a lot of things you hold on to with a deathlike grip. If you don't let go of some of the things you hold so tightly they will drag you down to hell. He would have you let go some of the things you pay taxes on, but don't own, and he would make you let go of money to pay taxes on some that you do own. Some people are so busy muckraking that they will lose a crown of glory hereafter. If God had your hands, how many countless tears you would wash away. A friend of mine bought a typewriter, and when he tried to use it his fingers seemed to be all sticks, but now he can write forty-five words a minute. Let God have your hands and he will make them do things that would make the angels wonder and applaud.

A young man went down to Thomasville, Alabama, and while there was invited to a dress ball—or rather an undress ball, if what I have read about such affairs properly describes the uniforms. A young lady—a young lady with eyes like the dove and with beautiful tresses—came up to him and said to the young man, "Won't you pledge a glass of champagne with me?"

The young man thanked her, but said: "No, I don't drink."

"Not with me?" she said, and smiled; and he repeated his answer, "No."

Then she said: "If I had thought you would refuse me I would not have asked you and exposed myself to the embarrassment of a refusal. I did not suppose you would think me bold for speaking to you in this way, and I thought you might be lonely."

A little later she came back to him and repeated her invitation. Again he said: "No."

Others came up and laughed. He took it and hesitated. She smiled at him and he gave in and drank the champagne, then drank another glass and another, until he was flushed with it. Then he danced.

At two o'clock the next morning a man with a linen duster over his other clothes walked back upon the railroad-station platform, waiting for a train for the North; and as he walked he would exclaim, "Oh, God!" and would pull a pint flask from his pocket and drink. "My God," he would say, "what will Mother say?" Four mouths later in his home in Vermont, with his weeping parents by him and with four strong men to hold him down, he died of delirium tremens.

The Epworth League's motto is: "Look up, lift up." But you'll never lift much up unless God has hold of your hands. Unless he has, you will never put your hands deep in your pocket, up to the elbows, and bring them up full of money for his cause. A man who was about to be baptized took out his watch and laid it aside; then he took out his knife and bank book and laid them aside.

"Better give me your pocketbook to put aside for you," said the minister.

"No," said the man, "I want it to be baptized, too."

There's no such thing as a bargain-counter religion. Pure and undefiled religion will do more when God has something besides pennies to work with. God doesn't run any excursions to heaven. You must pay the full fare. Your religion is worth just what it costs you. If you get religion and then lie down and go to sleep, your joints will get as Rip Van Winkle's did, and you'll never win the religious marathon.

A man said to his wife that he had heard the preacher say that religion is worth just what it costs, and that he had determined to give more for religion and to deny himself as well. "What will you give up?" she asked. He said that he would give up coffee—for he dearly loved coffee—used to drink several cups at every meal, the very best. She said that she would give up something, too—that she would give up tea. Then their daughter said she would give up some of her little pleasures, and the father turned to his son Tom, who was shoveling mashed potatoes covered with chicken gravy, into his mouth. He said, "I'll give up salt mackerel. I never did like the stuff, anyway."

There are too many salt-mackerel people like that in the pews of our churches today. They will take something that they don't like, and that nobody else will have, and give it to the Lord. That's isn't enough for God. He wants the best we have.

God wants your body with blood in it. Cain's altar was bigger than Abel's, but it had nothing valuable on it, while Abel's had real blood. God rejected Cain's and accepted Abel's. God turns down the man who merely lives a moral life and does not accept the religion of Jesus Christ. You must come with Jesus' blood. How thankful you are depends on how much you are willing to sacrifice.

I don't believe that the most honored angel in heaven has such a chance as we have. Angels can't suffer. They can't make sacrifices. They can claim that they love God, but we can prove it.

What would you think of a soldier if when he was ordered "Present arms," he would answer, "Tomorrow"; if he would say, "When the man next to me does"; if he would say, "When I get a new uniform?" "Present"—that means now. It is in the present tense. God wants us to make a present of our bodies to him—because we love him.

A little girl showed a man some presents she had received and he asked her, "How long may you keep them?"

"How long?" she answered. "Why, they were given to me. They are mine!"

Many a man gives his boy a colt or a calf, then when it has grown to a horse or a crow he sells it and pockets the money. Some of you fellows need to do a little thinking along that line. When we give our bodies, they ought to be His for keeps.

If when you make a present you do not mean to give it outright, you are not honest. "Will a man rob God?" You bet he will—a heap quicker than he will rob any one else.

Your body, that takes the head as well as hands. God wants brains as well as bones and muscles. We ought to do our best thinking for God. God is in the greatest business there is, and he wants the best help he can get. Some of you old deacons and elders make me sick. If you used such methods in business as you do in the work of the Church the sheriff's sale flag would soon be hanging outside your door. I don't ask any of you business men to curtail any of your business activities, but I do ask that you give more of your energy to the things of religion. You want to use good business methods in religion. The Republicans and the Democrats and the Socialists use good business methods in politics. The farmer who hasn't any sense is still plowing with a forked stick. The farmer who has sense uses a modern plow. Use common sense.

Bishop Taylor promised God that he would do as much hard thinking and planning for him as he would do for another man for money. He did it. So did Wesley and Whitefield and Savonarola, and look what they did for God! If there is any better way of doing God's business than there was one hundred years ago, for God's sake do it! He's entitled to the best there is. This thing of just ringing the church bell to get people to come in is about played out. In business, if they have a machine that is out of date and doesn't produce good results, it goes onto the scrap heap. If a man can produce a machine that can enlarge the product or better it, that machine is adopted at once. But in religion we have the same old flintlock guns, smooth-bore; the same old dips and tallow candles; the same old stage coaches over corduroy roads; and if a protest is made some of you will roll your eyes as if you had on a hair shirt, and say: "Surely this is not the Lord's set time for work." I tell you any time is God's time. Now is God's time. It was God's time to teach us about electricity long before Franklin discovered it, but nobody had sense enough to learn.

It was God's time to give us the electric light long before Edison invented it, but nobody had sense enough to understand it. It was God's set time to give us the steam engine long before Watt watched the kettle boil and saw it puff the lid off, but nobody had sense enough to grasp the idea.

If God Almighty only had possession of your mouths, he'd stop your lying. If he had your mouths he'd stop your knocking. If he had your mouths, he'd stop your misrepresentations. If he had your mouths, he'd stop your backbiting. If he had your mouths, he'd stop your slanders. There would be no criticizing, no white lies, no black lies, no social lies, no talking behind backs.

If God had your mouths, so much money wouldn't go up in tobacco smoke or out in tobacco spit. If God had your mouths, there would be no thousands of dollars a year spent for whisky, beer, and wine. You wouldn't give so much to the devil and you would give more to the Church. Many of you church pillars wouldn't be so noisy in politics and so quiet in religion. So many of you fellows wouldn't yell like Comanche Indians at a ratification meeting and sit like a bump on a log in prayer meeting.

If God had our eyes he'd bring the millennium. His eyes run to and fro through the world seeking for men to serve him; and if he had our eyes, how our eyes would run to and fro looking for ways to help bring men to Christ. How hard it would be for sinners to get away. We would be looking for drunkards and the prostitutes and down-and-outs to lift and save them. How many sorrowful hearts we would find and soothe, how many griefs we would alleviate! Great God! How little you are doing. Don't you feel ashamed? Aren't you looking for a knot hole to crawl through? If God had our eyes how many would stop looking at a lot of things that make us proud and unclean and selfish and critical and unchristian.

God wants you to give your body. Are you afraid to give it to him? Are you afraid of the doctor when you are sick? Your body—that thing that sits out there in the seat, that thing that sits up there in the choir and sings, that thing that sits there and writes editorials, that body which can show Jesus Christ to fallen sons of Adam better than any angel—that's what God wants. God wants you to bring it to him and say: "Take it, God, it's yours." If he had your body, dissipation, overeating and undersleeping would stop, for the body is holy ground. We dare not abuse it.

A friend of mine paid $10,000 for a horse. He put him in a stable and there the animal had caretakers attending him day and night, who rubbed him down, and watched his feet to take care that they should not be injured, and put mosquito netting on the windows, and cooled him with electric fans, and sprinkled his oats and his hay. They wanted to keep him in shape, for he was worth $10,000 and they wanted him for the race track. Give your body to God, and the devil will be welcome to anything he can find.

God wants your body as a living sacrifice, not a dead one. There are too many dead ones. A time was when God was satisfied with a dead sacrifice. Under old Jewish law a dead sheep would do. He wants my body now when I'm alive and not when I am dead and the undertaker is waiting to carry it out to the cemetery. The day of that dispensation is past, and now he wants you, a living sacrifice, a real sacrifice. A traveling man who wants to make his wife a present, and sits up all night in the train instead of taking a berth for three dollars and uses the three dollars to buy a present for his wife, makes a real sacrifice for her. There never was a victory without sacrifice. Socrates advanced the doctrine of immortality and died with a cup of poisoned hemlock. Jesus Christ paid with a crown of thorns. Abraham Lincoln paid with a bullet in his body. If you mean to give yourself as a sacrifice to God, get out and work for him. Ask men to come to him.

"A holy sacrifice." Some men shy at that word "holy" like a horse at an automobile. Holy vessels were set apart for use in the worship of God. To be holy is to be set apart for God's use—that's all. To be holy isn't to be long-faced and never smile.

"Acceptable unto the Lord." If that were true then this old desert would blossom like Eden. If that were taken as our watchword, what a stampede of short yardsticks, shrunken measures, light weights, adulterated foods, etc., there would be!

What a stopping of the hitting up of booze! There would be no more living in sin and keeping somebody on the side, no more of you old deacons coming down the aisles stroking your whiskers and renting your buildings for houses of ill fame, and newspapers would stop carrying ads for whisky and beer.

"Your reasonable service." God never asks anything unreasonable. He is never exacting. He only asks rights when he asks you to forsake sin. A man must be an idiot if he does not see that man is unreasonable when unrighteous. God never made a law to govern you that you wouldn't have made if you had known as much as God knows. You don't know that much and never can, so the only sensible thing to do is to obey God's laws. Faith never asks explanation.

God asks some things that are hard, but never any that are unreasonable. I beseech you, brethren. It was hard for Abraham to take his son up on the mountain and prepare to offer him up as a sacrifice to God, but God had a reason. Abraham understands tonight, and Abraham is satisfied. It was hard for Joseph to be torn from his own people and to be sold into Egypt and to be lied about by that miserable woman, torn from his mother and father, but God had a reason. Joseph knows tonight, and Joseph is satisfied. It was hard for Moses to lead the Jews from Egypt, following the cloud by day and the pillar of fire by night and make that crossing of the Red Sea, only to have God call him up to Mount Pisgah and show him the Promised Land and say: "Moses, you can't go in." It was hard, but God had a reason. Moses understands tonight, and Moses is satisfied. It was hard for Job to lose his children and all that he possessed and to be afflicted with boils, and to be so miserable that only his wife remained with him. But God had a reason. Job understands tonight, and Job is satisfied.

It was a hard thing God asked of Saul of Tarsus—to bear witness to him at Rome and Ephesus, to face those jeering heathen, to suffer imprisonment and be beaten with forty stripes save one, and finally to put his head on the block and have it severed by the order of old Nero, but God had a reason. Paul understands tonight, and Paul is satisfied. It was a hard thing God asked of Jesus—to leave the songs of the angels and the presence of the redeemed and glorified and come down to earth and be born amid the malodors of a stable, and be forced to flee from post to post, and dispute with the learned doctors in the temple at twelve years of age and confute them, and to still the storm and the troubled waters, and to say to the blind, "Be whole," and finally to be betrayed by one of his own followers and to be murdered through a conspiracy of Jews and Gentiles; but now he sits on the throne with the Father, awaiting the time to judge the world. Jesus understands and Jesus is satisfied.

It was a hard thing for me when God told me to leave home and go out into the world to preach the gospel and be vilified and libeled and have my life threatened and be denounced, but when my time comes, when I have preached my last sermon, and I can go home to God and the Lamb, he'll say, "Bill, this was the reason." I'll know what it all meant, and I'll say "I'm satisfied, God, I'm satisfied."

Booze

ere we have one of the strangest scenes in all the Gospels. Two men, possessed of devils, confront Jesus, and while the devils are crying out for Jesus to leave them, he commands the devils to come out, and the devils obey the command of Jesus. The devils ask permission to enter into a herd of swine feeding on the hillside. This is the only record we have of Jesus ever granting the petition of devils, and he did it for the salvation of men.

Then the fellows that kept the hogs went back to town and told the peanut-brained, weasel-eyed, hog-jowled, beetle-browed, bull-necked lobsters that owned the hogs, that "a long-haired fanatic from Nazareth, named Jesus, has driven the devils out of some men and the devils have gone into the hogs, and the hogs into the sea, and the sea into the hogs, and the whole bunch is dead."

And then the fat, fussy old fellows came out to see Jesus and said that he was hurting their business. A fellow says to me, "I don't think Jesus did a nice thing."

You don't know what you are talking about.

Down in Nashville, Tennessee, I saw four wagons going down the street, and they were loaded with stills, and kettles, and pipes.

"What's this?" I said.

"United States revenue officers, and they have been in the moonshine district and confiscated the illicit stills, and they are taking them down to the government scrap heap."

Jesus Christ was God's revenue officer. Now the Jews were forbidden to eat pork, but Jesus Christ came and found that crowd buying and selling and dealing in pork, and confiscated the whole business, and he kept within the limits of the law when he did it. Then the fellows ran back to those who owned the hogs to tell what had befallen them and those hog-owners said to Jesus: "Take your helpers and hike. You are hurting our business." And they looked into the sea and the hogs were bottom side up, but Jesus said, "What is the matter?"

And they answered, "Leave our hogs and go." A fellow says it is rather a strange request for the devils to make, to ask permission to enter into hogs. I don't know—if I were a devil I would rather live in a good, decent hog then in lots of men. If you will drive the hog out you won't have to carry slop to him, so I will try to help you get rid of the hog.

And they told Jesus to leave the country. They said: "You are hurting our business."

"Have you no interest in manhood?"

"We have no interest in that; just take your disciples and leave, for you are hurting our business."

That is the attitude of the liquor traffic toward the Church, and State, and Government, and the preacher that has the backbone to fight the most damnable, corrupt institution that ever wriggled out of hell and fastened itself on the public.

I am a temperance Republican down to my toes. Who is the man that fights the whisky business in the South? It is the Democrats! They have driven the business from Kansas, they have driven it from Georgia and Maine and Mississippi and North Carolina and North Dakota and Oklahoma and Tennessee and West Virginia. And they have driven it out of 1,756 counties. And it is the rock-ribbed Democratic South that is fighting the saloon. They started this fight that is sweeping like fire over the United States. You might as well try and dam Niagara Falls with toothpicks as to stop the reform wave sweeping our land. The Democratic party of Florida has put a temperance plank in its platform and the Republican party would nail that plank in their platform if they thought it would carry the election. It is simply a matter of decency and manhood, irrespective of politics. It is prosperity against poverty, sobriety against drunkenness, honesty, against thieving, heaven against hell. Don't you want to see men sober? Brutal, staggering men transformed into respectable citizens? "No, said the saloon-keeper, to hell with men. We are interested in our business, we have no interest in humanity."

After all is said that can be said upon the liquor traffic, its influence is degrading upon the individual, the family, politics and business, and upon everything that you touch in this old world. For the time has long gone by when there is any ground for arguments as to its ill effects. All are agreed on that point. There is just one prime reason why the saloon has not been knocked into hell, and that is the false statement that "the saloons are needed to help lighten the taxes." The saloon business has never paid, and it has cost fifty times more than the revenue derived from it.

I challenge you to show me where the saloon has ever helped business, education, church, morals or anything we hold dear.

The wholesale and retail trade in Iowa pays every year at least $500,-000 in licenses. Then if there were no drawback it ought to reduce the taxation twenty-five cents per capita. If the saloon is necessary to pay the taxes, and if they pay $500,000 in taxes, it ought to reduce them twenty-five cents a head. But no, the whisky business has increased taxes $1,000,000 instead of reducing them, and I defy any whisky man on God's dirt to show me one town that has the saloon where the taxes are lower than where they do not have the saloon. I defy you to show me an instance.

Listen! Seventy-five per cent of our idiots come from intemperate parents; eighty percent of the paupers, eighty-two percent of the crime is committed by men under the influence of liquor; ninety per cent of the adult criminals are whisky-made. The Chicago Tribune kept track for ten years and found that 53,556 murders were committed by men under the influence of liquor.

Archbishop Ireland, the famous Roman Catholic, of St. Paul, said of social crime today, that "seventy-five percent is caused by drink, and eighty percent of the poverty."

I go to a family and it is broken up, and I say, "What caused this?" Drink! I step up to a young man on the scaffold and say, "What brought you here?" Drink! Whence all the misery and sorrow corruption? Invariably it is drink.

Five points, in New York, was a spot as near like hell as any spot on earth. There are five streets that run to this point, and right in the middle was an old brewery and the streets on either side were lined with grog shops. The newspapers turned a searchlight on the district, and the first thing they had to do was to buy the old brewery and turn it into a mission.

The saloon is the sun of all villainies. It is worse than war or pestilence. It is the crime of cities. It is the parent of crimes and the mother of sins. It is the appalling source of misery and crime in the land. And to license such an incarnate fiend of hell is the dirtiest, low-down, damnable business on top of this old earth. There is nothing to be compared to it.

The legislature of Illinois appropriated $6,000,000 in 1908 to take care of the insane people in the state, and the whisky business produces seventy-five percent of the insane. That is what you go down in your pockets for to help support. Do away with the saloons and you will close these institutions. The saloons makes them necessary, and they make the poverty and fill the jails and the penitentiaries. Who has to pay the bills? The landlord who doesn't get the rent because the money goes for whisky; the butcher and the grocer and the charitable person who takes pity on the children of drunkards, and the taxpayer who supports the insane asylums and other institutions, that the whisky business keeps full of human wrecks.

Do away with the cursed business and you will not have to put up to support them. Who gets the money? The saloon-keepers and the brewers, and the distillers, while the whisky fills the land with misery, and poverty, and wretchedness, and disease, and death, and damnation, and it is being authorized by the will of the sovereign people.

You say that "people will drink anyway." Not by my vote. You say, "Men will murder their wives anyway." Not by my vote. You are the sovereign people, and what are you going to do about it?

Let me assemble before your minds the bodies of the drunken dead, who crawl away "into the jaws of death, into the mouth of hell," and then out of the valley of the shadow of drink let me call the appertaining motherhood, and wifehood, and childhood, and let their tears rain down upon their purple faces. Do you think that would stop the curse of the liquor traffic? No! No!

In these days when the question of saloon or no saloon is at the fore in almost every community, one hears a good deal about what is called "personal liberty." These are fine, large, mouth-filling words, and they certainly do sound first rate; but when you get right down and analyze them in the light of common old horse-sense, you will discover that in their application to the present controversy they mean just about this: "Personal liberty" is for the man who, if he has the inclination and the price, can stand up at the bar and fill his hide so full of red liquor that he is transformed for the time being into an irresponsible, dangerous, evilsmelling brute. But "personal liberty" is not for his patient, long-suffering wife, who has to endure with what fortitude she may his blows and curses; nor is it for his children, who, if they escape his in-sane rage, are yet robbed of every known joy and privilege of child-hood, and too often grow up neglected, uncared for and vicious as the result of their surroundings and the example before them. "Personal liberty" is not for the sober, industrious citizen who from the proceeds of honest toil and orderly living, has to pay, willingly or not, the tax bills which pile up as a direct result of drunkenness, disorder and pov-erty, the items of which are written in the records of every police court and poorhouse in the land; nor is "personal liberty" for the good woman who goes abroad in the town only at the risk of being shot down by some drink-crazed creature. This rant about "personal lib-erty" as an argument has no leg to stand upon.

Now, in 1913 the corn crop was 2,373,000,000 bushels, and it was valued at $1,660,000,000. Secretary Wilson says that the breweries use less than two percent; I will say that they use two percent. That would make 47,000,000 bushels and at seventy cents a bushel that would be about $33,000,000. How many people are there in the United States? Ninety millions. Very well, then, that is thirty-six cents per capita. Then we sold out to the whisky business for thirty-six cents apiece—the price of a dozen eggs or a pound of butter. We are the cheapest gang this side of hell if we will do that kind of business.

Now listen! Last year the income of the United States government, and the cities and towns and counties, from the whisky business was $350,000,000. That is putting it liberally. You say that's a lot of money. Well, last year the workingmen spent $2,000,000,000 for drink, and it cost $1,200,000,000 to care for the judicial machinery. In other words, the whisky business cost us last year $3,400,000,000. I will subtract from that the dirty $350,000,000 which we got, and it leaves $3,050,000,000 in favor of knocking the whisky business out on purely a money basis. And listen! We spend $6,000,000,000 a year for our paupers and criminals, insane, orphans, feeble-minded, etc., and eighty-two percent of our criminals are whisky-made, and seventy-five percent of the paupers are whisky-made. The average factory hand earns $450 a year, and it costs us $1,200 a year to support each of our whisky criminals. There are 326,000 enrolled criminals in the United States and 80,000 in jails and penitentiaries. Three-fourths were sent there because of drink, and then they have the audacity to say the saloon is needed for money revenue. Never was there a baser lie.

"But," says the whisky fellow, "we would lose trade, the farmer would not come to town to trade." You lie. I am a farmer. I was born and raised on a farm and I have the malodors of the barnyard on me today. Yes, sir. And when you say that you insult the best class of men on God's dirt. Say, when you put up the howl that if you don't have the saloons the farmer won't trade—say, Mr. Whisky Man, why do you dump money into politics and back the legislatures into the corner and fight to the last ditch to prevent the enactment of county local option? You know if the farmers were given a chance they would knock the whisky business into hell the first throw out of the box. You are afraid. You have cold feet on the proposition. You are afraid to give the farmer a chance. They are scared to death of you farmers.

I heard my friend ex-Governor Hanly, of Indiana, use the following illustrations:

"Oh, but," they say, "Governor, there is another danger to the local option, because it means a loss of market to the farmer. We are consumers of large quantities of grain in the manufacture of our products. If you drive us out of business you strike down that market and it will create a money panic in this country, such as you have never seen, if you do that." I might answer it by saying that less than two percent of the grain produced in this country is used for that purpose, but I pass that by. I want to debate the merit of the statement itself, and I think I can demonstrate in ten minutes to any thoughtful man, to any farmer, that the brewer who furnishes him a market for a bushel of corn is not his benefactor, or the benefactor of any man, from an economic standpoint. Let us see. A farmer brings to the brewer a bushel of corn. He finds a market for it. He gets fifty cents and goes his way, with the statement of the brewer ringing in his ears, that the brewer is the benefactor. But you haven't got all the factors in the problem, Mr. Brewer, and you cannot get a correct solution of a problem without all the factors in the problem. You take the farmer's bushel of corn, brewer or distiller, and you brew and distill from it four and one-half gallons of spirits. I don't know how much he dilutes them before he puts them on the market. Only the brewer, the distiller and God know. The man who drinks it doesn't, but if he doesn't dilute it at all, he puts on the market four and a half gallons of intoxicating liquor, thirty-six pints. It will take too long. But I want to trace three of them and I will give you no imaginary stories plucked from the brain of an excited orator. I will take instances from the judicial pages of the Supreme Court and the Circuit Court judges' reports in Indiana and in Illinois to make my case.

Several years ago in the city of Chicago a young man of good parents, good character, one Sunday crossed the street and entered a saloon, open against the law. He found there boon companions. There were laughter, song, and jest and much drinking. After awhile, drunk, insanely drunk, his money gone, he was kicked into the street. He found his way across to his mother's home. He importuned her for money to buy more drink. She refused him. He seized from the sideboard a revolver and ran out into the street and with the expressed determination of entering the saloon and getting more drink, money or no money. His fond mother followed him into the street. She put her hand upon him in a loving restraint. He struck it from him in anger, and then his sister came and added her entreaty in vain. And then a neighbor, whom he knew, trusted and respected, came and put his hand on him in gentleness and friendly kindness, but in an insanity of drunken rage he raised the revolver and shot his friend dead in his blood upon the street. There was a trial; he was found guilty of murder. He was sentenced to life imprisonment, and when the little mother heard the verdict—a frail little bit of a woman—she threw up her hands and fell in a swoon. In three hours she was dead.

In the streets of Freeport, Illinois, a young man of good family became involved in a controversy with a lewd woman of the town. He went in a drunken frenzy to his father's home, armed himself with a deadly weapon and set out for the city in search of the woman with whom he had quarreled. The first person he met upon the public square in the city, in the daylight, in a place where she had a right to be, was one of the most refined and cultured women of Freeport. She carried in her arms her babe—motherhood and babyhood, upon the streets of Freeport in the daytime, where they had a right to be—but this young man in his drunken insanity mistook her for the woman he sought and shot her dead upon the streets with her babe in her arms. He was tried and Judge Ferand, in sentencing him to life imprisonment said: "You are the seventh man in two years to be sentenced for murder while intoxicated."

In the city of Anderson, you remember the tragedy in the Blake home. A young man came home intoxicated, demanding money of his mother. She refused it. He seized from the wood box a hatchet and killed his mother and then robbed her. You remember he fled. The officer of the law pursued him and brought him back. An indictment was read upon him charging him with the murder of the mother who had given him his birth, of her who had gone down into the valley of the shadow of death to give him life, of her who had looked down into his blue eyes and thanked God for his life. And he said, "I am guilty; I did it all." And Judge McClure sentenced him to life imprisonment.

Now I have followed probably three of the thirty-six pints of the farmer's product of a bushel of corn and the three of them have struck down seven lives, the three boys who committed the murders, the three persons who were killed and the little mother who died of a broken heart. And now, I want to know, my farmer friend, if this has been a good commercial transaction for you? You sold a bushel of corn; you found a market; you got fifty cents; but a fraction of this product struck down seven lives, all of whom would have been consumers of your products for their life expectancy. And do you mean to say that is a good economic transaction to you? That disposes of the market question until it is answered; let no man argue further.

And say, my friends New York City's drink bill is $365,000,000 a year, $1,000,000 a day. Listen a minute. That is four times the annual output of gold, and six times the value of all the silver mined in the United States. And in New York there is one saloon for every thirty families. The money spent in New York by the working people for drink in ten years would buy every working man in New York a beautiful home, allowing $3,500 for house and lot. It would take fifty persons one year to count the money in $1 bills, and they would cover

10,000 acres of ground. That is what the people in New York dump into the whisky hole in one year. And then you wonder why there is poverty and crime, and that the country is not more prosperous.

The whisky gang is circulating a circular about Kansas City, Kansas. I defy you to prove a statement in it. Kansas City is a town of 100,000 population, and temperance went into effect July 1, 1905. Then they had 250 saloons, 200 gambling halls and 60 houses of ill fame. The population was largely foreign, and inquiries have come from Germany, Sweden and Norway, asking the influence of the enforcement of the prohibitory law.

At the end of one year the president of one of the largest banks in that city, a man who protested against the enforcement of the prohibitory law on the ground that it would hurt business, found that his bank deposits increased $1,700,000, and seventy-two percent of the deposits were from men who had never saved a cent before, and forty-two percent came from men who never had a dollar in the bank, but because the saloons were driven out they had a chance to save, and the people who objected on the grounds that it would injure business found an increase of 209 percent in building operations; and, furthermore, there were three times as many people seeking investment, and court expenses decreased $25,000 in one year.

Who pays to feed and keep the gang you have in jail? Why, you go down in your sock and pay for what the saloon has dumped there. They don't do it. Mr. Whisky Man, why don't you go down and take a picture of wrecked and blighted homes, and of insane asylums, with gibbering idiots. Why don't you take a picture of that?

At Kansas City, Kansas, before the saloons were closed, they were getting ready to build an addition to the jail. Now the doors swing idly on the hinges and there is nobody to lock in the jails. And the commissioner of the Poor Farm says there is a wonderful falling off of old men and women coming to the Poor House, because their sons and daughters are saving their money and have quit spending it for drink. And they had to employ eighteen new school teachers for 600 boys and girls, between the ages of twelve and eighteen, that had never gone to school before because they had to help a drunken father support the family. And they have just set aside $200,000 to build a new school house, and the bonded indebtedness was reduced $245,000 in one year without the saloon revenue. And don't you know another thing: In 1906, when they had the saloon, the population, according to the directory, was 89,655. According to the census of 1907 the population was 100,835, or an increase of twelve percent in one year, without the grog-shop. In two years the bank deposits increased $3,930,000.

You say, drive out the saloon and you kill business—Ha! ha! "Blessed are the dead that die in the Lord."

I tell you, gentlemen, the American home is the dearest heritage of the people, for the people, and when a man can go from home in the morning with the kisses of his wife and children on his lips, and come back at night with an empty bucket to a happy home, that man is a better man, whether white or black. Whatever takes away the comforts of home—whatever degrades that man or woman—whatever invades the sanctity of the home, is the deadliest foe to the home, to church, to state and school, and the saloon is the deadliest foe to the home, the church and the state, on top of God Almighty's dirt. And if all the combined forces of hell should assemble in conclave, and with them all the men on earth that hate and despite God, and purity, and virtue—if all the scum of the earth could mingle with the denizens of hell to try to think of the deadliest institution to home, to church and state, I tell you, sir, the combined hellish intelligence could not conceive of or bring an institution that could touch the hem of the garment of the open licensed saloon to damn the home and manhood, and womanhood, and business and every other good thing on God's earth.

In the Island of Jamaica the rats increased so that they destroyed the crops, and they introduced a mongoose, which is a species of the coon. They have three breeding seasons a year and there are twelve to fifteen in each brood, and they are deadly enemies of the rats. The result was that the rats disappeared and there was nothing more for the mongoose to feed upon, so they attacked the snakes, and the frogs, and the lizards that fed upon the insects, with the result that the insects increased and they stripped the gardens, eating up the onions and the lettuce and then the mongoose attacked the sheep and the cats, and the puppies, and calves and the geese. Now Jamaica is spending hundreds of thousands of dollars to get rid of the mongoose.

The American mongoose is the open licensed saloon. It eats the carpets off the floor and the clothes from your back, your money out of the bank, and it eats up character, and it goes on until at last it leaves a stranded wreck in the home, a skeleton of what was once brightness and happiness.

There were some men playing cards on the railroad train. and one fellow pulled out a whisky flask and passed it about, and when it came to the drummer he said, "No." "What," they said, "have you got on the water wagon?" and they all laughed at him. He said, "You can laugh if you want to, but I was born with an appetite for drink, and for years I have taken from five to ten glasses per day, but I was at home in Chicago not long ago and I have a friend who has a pawn shop there. I was in there when in came a young fellow with ashen cheeks and a wild look on his face. He came up trembling, threw down a little package and said, 'Give me ten cents." And what do you think was in that package? It was a pair of baby shoes.

"My friend said, 'No, I cannot take them.'

" 'But,' he said, 'give me a dime. I must have a drink?'

"No, take them back home, your baby will need them.'

"And the poor fellow said, 'My baby is dead, and I want a drink.' "

Boys, I don't blame you for the lump that comes up in your throat. There is no law, divine or human, that the saloon respects. Lincoln said, "If slavery is not wrong, nothing is wrong." I say, if the saloon, with its train of diseases, crime and misery, is not wrong, then nothing on earth is wrong. If the fight is to be won we need men—men that will fight—the Church, Catholic and Protestant, must fight it or run away, and thank God she will not run away, but fight to the last ditch.

Who works the hardest for his money, the saloon man or you?

Who has the most money Sunday morning, the saloon man or you?

The saloon comes as near being a rat hole for a wage earner to dump his wages in as anything you can find. The only interest it pays is red eyes and foul breath, and the loss of health. You go in with money and you come out with empty pockets. You go in with character and you come out ruined. You go in with a good position and you lose it. You lost your position in the bank, or in the cab of the locomotive. And it pays nothing back but disease and damnation and gives an extra dividend in delirium tremens and a free pass to hell. And then it will let your wife be buried in the potter's field and your children go to the asylum, and yet you walk out and say the saloon is a good institution, when it is the dirtiest thing on earth. It hasn't one leg to stand on and has nothing to commend it to a decent man, not one thing.

"But," you say, "we will regulate it by high license." Regulate what by high license? You might as well try and regulate a powder mill in hell. Do you want to pay taxes in boys, or dirty money? A man that will sell out to that dirty business I have no use for. See how absurd their arguments are. If you drink Bourbon in a saloon that pays $1,000 a year license, will it eat your stomach less if you drink it in a saloon that pays $500 license? Is it going to have any different effect on you, whether the gang pays $500 or $1,000 license? No. It will make no difference whether you drink it over a mahogany counter or a pine counter—it will have the same effect on you; it will damn you. So there is no use talking about it.

In some insane asylums, do you know what they do? When they want to test some patient to see whether he has recovered his reason, they have a room with a faucet in it, and a cement floor, and the give the patient a mop and tell him to mop up the floor. And if he has sense enough to turn off the faucet and mop up the floor they will parole him, but should he let the faucet run, they know that he is crazy.

Well, that is what you are trying to do. You are trying to mop it up with taxes and insane asylums and jails and Keeley cures, and reformatories. The only thing to do is to shut off the source of supply.

A man was delivering a temperance address at a fair grounds and a fellow came up to him and said: "Are you the fellow that gave a talk on temperance?"

"Yes."

"Well, I think the managers did a dirty piece of business to let you give a lecture on temperance. You have hurt my business and my business is a legal one."

"You are right there," said the lecturer, "they did do a mean trick; I would complain to the officers." And he took up a premium list and said: "By the way, I see there is a premium of so much offered for the best horse and cow and butter. What business are you in?"

"I'm in the liquor business."

"Well, I don't see that they offer any premiums for your business. You ought to go down and compel them to offer on the list $25 for the best wrecked home, $15 for the best bloated bum that you can show, and $10 for the finest specimen of broken-hearted wife, and they ought to give $25 for the finest specimens of thieves and gamblers you can trot out. You can bring out the finest looking criminals. If you have something that is good trot it out. You ought to come in competition with farmers, with his stock, and the fancy work, and the canned fruit."

As Dr. Howard said: "I tell you that the saloon is a coward. It hides itself behind stained-glass doors and opaque windows, and sneaks its customers in at a blind door, and it keeps a sentinel to guard the door from the officers of the law, and it marks its wares with false bill-of-lading, and offers to ship green goods to you and marks them with the name of wholesome articles of food so people won't know what is being sent you. And so vile did that business get that the legislature of Indiana passed a law forbidding them to send whisky through the mails.

I tell you it strikes in the night. It fights under cover of darkness and assassinates the characters that it cannot damn, and it lies about you. It attacks defenseless womanhood and childhood. The saloon is a coward. It is a thief; it is not an ordinary court offender that steals your money; but it robs you of manhood and leaves you in rags and takes away your friends, and it robs your family. It impoverishes your children and it brings insanity and suicide. It will take the shirt off your back and it will steal the coffin from a dead child and yank the last crust of bread out of the hand of the starving child; it will take the last bucket of coal out of your cellar, and the last cent out of your pocket, and will send you home bleary-eyed and staggering to your wife and children. It will steal the milk from the breast of the mother and leave her with nothing with which to feed her infant. It will take the virtue from your daughter. It is the dirtiest, most low-down damnable business that ever crawled out of the pit of hell. It is a sneak, and a thief and a coward.

It is an infidel. It has no faith in God; has no religion. It would close every church in the land. It would bring hang its beer signs on the abandoned altars. It would close every public school. It respects the thief and it esteems the blasphemer; it fills the prisons and penitentiaries. It despises heaven, hates love, scorns virtue. It tempts the passions. Its music is the song of siren. Its sermons are a collection of lewd,

/ile stories. It wraps a mantle about the mopes of this world and that to come. Its tables are full of the vilest literature. It is the moral clearing house for rot, and damnation, and poverty, and insanity, and it wrecks homes and blights lives today.

The saloon is a liar. It promises good cheer and sends sorrow. It promises health and causes disease. It promises prosperity and sends poverty. It promises happiness and sends misery. Yes, it sends the husband home with a lie on his lips to his wife; and the boy home with a lie on his lips to his mother; and it causes the employee to lie to his employer. It degrades. It is God's worst enemy and the devil's best friend. It spares neither youth nor old age. It is waiting with a dirty blanket for the baby to crawl into the world. It lies in wait for the unborn.

It cocks the highwayman's pistol. It puts the rope in the hands of the mob. It is the anarchist of the worlds, and its dirty red flag is dyed with the blood of women and children. It sent the bullet through the body of Lincoln; it nerved the arm that sent the bullets through Garfield and William McKinley. Yes, it is a murderer. Every plot that was ever hatched against the government and law, was born and bred, and crawled out of the grog-shop to damn this country.

I tell you that the curse of God Almighty is on the saloon. Legislatures are legislating against it. Decent society is barring it out. The fraternal brotherhoods are knocking it out. The Masons and Odd Fellows, and the Knights of Pythias and the A. O. U. W. are closing their doors to the whisky sellers. They don't want you wriggling your carcass in their lodges. Yes, sir, I tell you, the curse of God is on it. It is on the down grade. It is headed for hell, and, by the grace of God I am going to give it a push, with a whoop, for all I know how. Listen to me! I am going to show you how we burn up our money. It costs twenty cents to make a gallon of whisky: sold over the counter at ten cents a glass, it will bring four dollars.

"But," said the saloon-keeper, "Bill, you must figure on the strychnine and the cohienal, and other stuff they put in it, and it will bring nearer eight dollars."

Yes; it increases the heart beat thirty times more in a minute, when you consider the licorice and potash and log-wood and other poisons that are put in. I believe one cause for the unprecedented increase of crime is due to the poison put in the stuff nowadays to make it go as far as they can.

I am indebted to my friend, George B. Stuart, for some of the following points:

I will show you how your money is burned up. It costs twenty cents to make a gallon of whisky, sold over the counter at ten cents a glass, which brings four dollars. Listen, where does it go? Who gets the twenty cents? The farmer for his corn or rye. Who gets the rest? The United States government for collecting revenue, and the big corporations, and part is used to pave our streets and pay our police. I'll show you. I'm going to show you how it is burned up, and you don't need half sense to catch on, and if you don't understand just keep still and nobody will know the difference.

I say, "Hey, Colonel Politics, what is the matter with the country?"

He swells up like a poisoned pup and says to me, "Bill, why the silver bugbear. That's what is the matter with the country."

The total value of the silver produced in this country in 1912 was $38,000,000. Hear me! In 1912 the total value of the gold produced in this country was $93,000,000, and we dumped thirty-six times that much in the whisky hole and didn't fill it. What is the matter? The total value of all the gold and silver produced in 1912 was $132,000,000, and we dumped twenty-five times that amount in the whisky hole and didn't fill it.

What is the matter with the country, Colonel Politics? He swells up and says, "Mr. Sunday, Standpatism, sir."

I say, "You are an old windbag."

"Oh," says another, "revision of the tariff." Another man says, "Free trade; open the doors at the ports and let them pour the products in and we will put the trusts on the side-track."

Say, you come with me to every port of entry. Listen! In 1912 the total value of all the imports was $1,812,000,000, and we dumped that much in the whisky hole in twelve months and did not fill it.

"Oh," says a man, "let us court South America and Europe to sell our products. That's what is the matter; we are not exporting enough."

Last year the total value of all the exports was $2,362,000,000, and we dumped that amount in the whisky hole in one year and didn't fill it.

One time I was down in Washington and went to the United States treasury and said: "I wish you would let me go where you don't let the general public." And they took us around on the inside and we walked into a room about twenty feet long and fifteen feet wide and as many feet high, and I said, "What is this?"

"This is the vault that contains all of the national bank stock in the United States."

I said, "How much is here?"

They said, "$578,000,000."

And we dumped nearly four times the value of the national bank stock in the United States into the whisky hole last year, and we didn't fill the hole up at that. What is the matter? Say, whenever the day comes that all the Catholic and Protestant churches—just when the day comes when you will say to the whisky business: "You go to hell," that day the whisky business will go to hell. But you sit there, you old whisky-voting elder and deacon and vestryman, and you wouldn't strike your hands together on the proposition. It would stamp you an old hypocrite and you know it.

Say, hold on a bit. Have you got a silver dollar? I am going to show you how it is burned up. We have in this country 250,000 saloons, and allowing fifty feet frontage for each saloon it makes a street from New York to Chicago, and 5,000,000 men, women and children go daily into the saloon for drink. And marching twenty miles a day it would take thirty days to pass this building, and marching five abreast they would reach 590 miles. There they go; look at them!

On the first day of January, 500,000 of the young men of our nation entered the grog-shop and began a public career hellward, and on the 31st of December I will come back here and summon you people, and ring the bell and raise the curtain and say to the saloon and breweries: "On the first day of January, I gave you 500,000 of the brain and muscle of our land, and I want them back and have come in the name of the home and the church and school: father, mother, sister, sweetheart; give me back what I gave you. March out."

I count, and 165,000 have lost their appetites and have become muttering, bleary-eyed drunkards, wallowing in their own excrement, and I say "What is it I hear, a funeral dirge?" What is that procession? A funeral procession 3,000 miles long and 110,000 hearses in the procession. One hundred and ten thousand men die drunkards in the land of the free and home of the brave! Listen! In an hour twelve men die drunkards, 300 a day and 110,000 a year. One man will leap in front of a train, another will plunge from the dock into the lake, another will throw his hands to his head and life will end. Another will cry, "Mother," and his life will go out like a burnt match.

I stand in front of the jails and count the whisky criminals. They say, "Yes, Bill, I fired the bullet." "Yes, I backed my wife into the corner and beat her life out. I am waiting for the scaffold; I am waiting." "I am waiting," says another, "to slip into hell." On, on, it goes. Say, let me summon the wifehood, and the motherhood, and the childhood and see the tears rain down the upturned faces. People, ears are too weak for those hellish drunkards. Everybody fall in. Come on, ready, forward, march. Right, left, here I come with all the drunkards. We will line up in front of a butcher shop. The butcher says. "What do you want, a piece of neck?"

"No; how much do I owe you?" "Three dollars." "Here's your dough. Now give me a porterhouse steak and a sirloin roast."

"Where did you get all that money?"

"Went to hear Bill and climbed on the water wagon."

"Hello! What do you want?"

"Beefsteak."

"What do you want?"

"Beefsteak."

We empty the shop and the butcher runs to the telephone. "Hey, Central, give me the slaughter house. Have you got any beef, any pork, any mutton?"

They strip the slaughter house, and then telephone to Swift and Armour, and Nelson Morris, and Cudahy, to send down trainloads of beefsteaks.

"The whole bunch has got on the water wagon."

And Swift and other big packers in Chicago say to their salesmen: "Buy beef, pork, and mutton."

The farmer sees the price of cattle and sheep jump up to three times their value. Let me take the money you dump into the whisky hole and buy beefsteaks with it. I will show what is the matter with America. I think the liquor business is the dirtiest, rottenest business this side of hell.

Come on, are you ready? Fall in! We line up in front of a grocery store.

"What do you want?"

"Why, I want flour."

"What do you want?"

"Flour."

"Pillsbury, Minneapolis, 'Sleepy Eye'?"

"Yes, ship in trainloads of flour; send on fast mail schedule, with an engine in front, one behind and a Mogul in the middle."

"What's the matter?"

"Why, the workingmen have stopped spending their money for booze and have begun to buy flour."

The big mills tell their men to buy wheat and the farmers see the price jump to over $2 per bushel. What's the matter with the country? Why, the whisky gang has your money and you have an empty stomach, and yet you will walk up and vote for the dirty booze.

Come on, cut out the booze, boys. Get on the water wagon; get on for the sake of your wife and babies, and hit the booze a blow.

Come on, ready, forward, march! Right, left, halt! We are in front of a dry goods store.

"What do you want?"

"Calico."

"What do you want?"

"Calico."

"What do you want?"

"Calico."

"Calico; all right, come on." The stores are stripped.

Marshall Field, Carson, Pirie, Scott & Co., J. V. Farrell, send down calico. The whole bunch has voted out the saloons and we have such a demand for calico we don't know what to do. And the big stores telegraph to Fall River to ship calico, and the factories telegraph to buy cotton, and they tell their salesmen to buy cotton, and the cotton plantation man sees cotton jump up to $150 a bale.

What is the matter? Your children are going naked and the whisky gang has got your money. That's what's the matter with you. Don't listen to those old whisky-soaked politicians who say "stand pat on the saloon."

Come with me. Now, remember we have the whole bunch of booze fighters on the water wagon, and I'm going home now. Over there I was John, the drunken bum. The whisky gang got my dollar and I got the quart. Over here I am John on the water wagon. The merchant got my dollar and I have his meat, flour and calico, and I'm going home now. "Be it ever humble, there's no place like home without booze."

Wife comes out and says, "Hello, John, what have you got?"

"Two porterhouse steaks, Sally."

"What's that bundle, Pa?"

"Clothes to make you a new dress, Sis. Your mother has fixed your old one so often, it looks like a crazy quilt."

"And what have you there?"

"That's a pair of shoes for you, Tom; and here is some cloth to make you a pair of pants. Your mother has patched the old ones so often, they look like the map of the United States."

What's the matter with the country? We have been dumping into the whisky hole the money that ought to have been spent for flour, beef and calico, and we haven't the hole filled up yet.

A man comes along and says: "Are you a drunkard?"

"Yes, I'm a drunkard."

"Where are you going?"

"I am going to hell."

"Why?"

"Because the Good Book says: 'No drunkard shall inherit the kingdom of God,' so I am going to hell."

Another man comes along and I say: "Are you a church member?"

"Yes, I am a church member."

"Where are you going?"

"I am going to heaven."

"Did you vote for the saloon?"

"Yes."

"Then you shall go to hell."

Say, if the man that drinks the whisky goes to hell, the man that votes for the saloon that sold the whisky will go to hell. If the man that drinks the whisky goes to hell, and the man that sold the whisky to the men that drank it, goes to heaven, then the poor drunkard will have the right to stand on the brink of eternal damnation and put his arms around the pillar of justice, shake his fist in the face of the Almighty and say, "Unjust! Unjust!" If you vote for the dirty business you ought to go to hell as sure as you live, and I would like to fire the furnace while you are there.

Some fellow says, "Drive the saloon out and the buildings will be empty." Which would you rather have, empty buildings or empty jails, penitentiaries and insane asylums. You drink the stuff and what have you to say? You that vote for it, and you that sell it? Look at them painted on the canvas of your recollection.

What is the matter with this grand old country? I heard my friend, George Stuart, tell how he imagined that he walked up to a mill and said:

"Hello, there, what kind of a mill are you?"

"A sawmill."

"And what do you make?"

"We make boards out of logs."

"Is the finished product worth more than the raw material?"

"Yes."

"We will make laws for you. We must have lumber for houses."

He goes up to another mill and says:

"Hey, what kind of a mill are you?"

"A grist mill."

"What do you make?"

"Flour and meal out of wheat and corn."

"Is the finished product worth more than the raw material?"

"Yes."

"Then come on. We will make laws for you. We will protect you."

He goes up to another mill and says:

"What kind of a mill are you?"

"A paper mill."

"What do you make paper out of?"

"Straw and rags."

"Well, we will make laws for you. We must have paper on which to write notes and mortgages."

He goes up to another mill and says:

"Hey, what kind of a mill are you?"

"A gin mill."

"I don't like the looks nor the smell of you. A gin mill; what do you make: What kind of a mill are you?"

"A gin mill."

"What is your raw material?"

"The boys of America."

The gin mills of this country must have 2,000,000 boys or shut up shop. Say, walk down your streets, count the homes and every fifth home has to furnish a boy for a drunkard. Have you furnished yours? No. Then I have to furnish two to make up.

"What is your raw material?"

"American boys."

"Then I will pick up the boys and give them to you."

A man says, "Hold on, not my boy, he is mine."

Then I will say to you what saloon-keeper said to me when I protested, "I am not interested in boys; to hell with your boys." "Say, saloon gin mill, what is your finished product?"

"Bleary-eyed, low-down, staggering men and the scum of God's dirt."

Go to the jails, go to the insane asylums and the penitentiaries, and the homes for feeble-minded. There you will find the finished product for their dirty business. I tell you it is the worst business this side of hell, and you know it.

Listen! Here is an extract from the *Saturday Evening Post* of November 9, 1907, taken from a paper read by a brewer. You will say that a man didn't say it: "It appears from these facts that the success of our business lies in the creation of appetite among the boys. Men who have formed the habit scarcely ever reform, but they, like others, will die, and unless there are recruits made to take their places, our coffers will be empty, and I recommend to you that money be spent in creation of appetite will return in dollars to your tills after the habit is formed."

What is your raw material, saloons? American boys. Say, I would not give one boy for all the distilleries and saloons this side of hell. And they have to have 2,000,000 boys every generation. And then you tell me you are a man when you will vote for an institution like that. What do you want to do, pay taxes in money or in boys?

I feel like an old fellow in Tennessee who made his living by catching rattlesnakes. He caught one with fourteen rattles and put it in a box with a glass top. One day when he was sawing wood his little five-year-old boy, Jim, took the lid off and the rattler wiggled out and struck him in the cheek. He ran to his father and said, "The rattle has bit me." The father ran and chopped the rattler to pieces, and with his jack-knife he cut a chunk from the boy's cheek and then sucked and sucked at the wound to draw out the poison. He looked at little Jim, watched the pupils of his eyes dilate and watched him swell to three times his normal size, watched his lips become parched and cracked, and eyes roll, and little Jim gasped and died.

The father took him in his arms, carried him over by the side of the rattler, got on his knees and said, "O God, I would not give little Jim for all the rattlers that ever crawled over the Blue Ridge mountains."

And I would not give one boy for every dirty dollar you get from the hell-soaked liquor business or from every brewery and distillery this side of hell.

In a Northwest city a preacher sat at his breakfast table one Sunday morning. The door-bell rang; he answered it; and here stood a little boy, twelve years of age. He was on crutches, right leg off at the knee, shivering, and he said, "Please, sir, will you come up to the jail and talk and pray with papa? He murdered mamma. Papa was good and kind, but whisky did it, and I have to support my three little sisters. I sell newspapers and black boots. Will you go up and talk and pray with papa? And will you come home and be with us when they bring him back? The governor says we can have his body after they hang him."

The preacher hurried to the jail and talked and prayed with the man. He had no knowledge of what he had done. He said, "I don't blame the law, but it breaks my heart to think that my children must be left in a cold and heartless world. Oh, sir, whisky did it."

The preacher was at the little hut when up drove the undertaker's wagon and they carried out the pine coffin. They led the little boy up to the coffin, he leaned over and kissed his father and sobbed, and said to his sister, "Come on, sister, kiss papa's cheeks before they grow cold." And the little hungry, ragged, whisky orphans hurried to the coffin, shrieking in agony. Police, whose hearts were adamant, buried their faces in their hands and rushed from the house, and the preacher fell on his knees and lifted his clenched fist and tear-stained face and took an oath before God, and before the whisky orphans, that he would fight the cursed business until the undertaker carried him out in a coffin.

You men have a chance to show your manhood. Then in the name of your pure mother, in the name of your manhood, in the name of your wife and the poor innocent children that climb up on your lap and put their arms around your neck, in the name of all that is good and noble, fight the curse. Shall you men, who hold in your hands the ballot, and in that ballot hold the destiny of womanhood and childhood and manhood, shall you, the sovereign power, refuse to rally in the name of the defenseless men and women and native land? No.

I want every man to say, "God, you can count on me to protect my wife, my home, my mother and my children and the manhood of America."

By the mercy of God, which has given to you the unshaken and unshakable confidence of her you love, I beseech you, make a fight for the women who wait until the saloons spew out their husbands and their sons, and send them home maudlin, brutish, devilish, stinking, bleary-eyed, bloated-faced drunkards.

You say you can't prohibit men from drinking. Why, if Jesus Christ were here today some of you would keep on in sin just the same. But the law can be enforced against whisky just the same as it can be enforced against anything else, if you have honest officials to enforce it. Of course it doesn't probibit. There isn't a law on the books of the state that prohibits. We have laws against murder. Do they prohibit? We have laws against burglary. Do they prohibit? We have laws against arson, rape, but do they prohibit? Would you introduce a bill to repeal all the laws that do not prohibit? Any law will prohibit to a certain extent if honest officials enforce it. But no law will absolutely prohibit. We can make law against liquor prohibit as much as any law prohibits.

Or would you introduce a bill saying, if you pay $1,000 a year you can kill any one you don't like; or by paying $500 a year you can attack any girl you want to; or by paying $100 a year you can steal anything that suits you? That's what you do with the dirtiest, rottenest gang this side of hell. You say for so much a year you can have a license to make staggering, reeling drunken sots, murderers and thieves and vagabonds. You say, "Bill, you're too hard on the whisky." I don't agree. Not on your life. There was a fellow going along the pike and a farmer's dog ran snapping at him. He tried to drive it back with a pitchfork he carried, and failing to do so he pinned it to the ground with prongs. Out came the farmer: "Hey, why don't you use the other end of that fork?" He answered, "Why didn't the dog come at me with the other end?"

Personal liberty is not personal license. I dare not exercise personal liberty if it infringes on the liberty of others. Our forefathers did not fight and die for personal license but for personal liberty bounded by laws. Personal liberty is the liberty of a murderer, a burglar, a seducer, or a wolf that wants to remain in a sheep fold, or the weasel in a hen roost. You have no right to vote for an institution that is going to drag your sons and daughters to hell.

If you were the only persons in this city you would have a perfect right to drive your horse down the street at breakneck speed; you would have a right to make a race track out of the streets for your auto; you could build a glue factory in the public square. But when the population increases from one to 600,000 you can't do it. You say, "Why can't I run my auto? I own it. Why can't I run my horse? I own it. Why can't I build the slaughter house? I own the lot." Yes, but there are 600,000 people here now and other people have rights.

So law stands between you and your personal liberty, you miserable dog. You can't build a slaughter house in your front yard, because the law says you can't. As long as I am standing here on this platform I have personal liberty. I can swing my arms at will. But the minute any one else steps on the platform my personal liberty ceases. It stops just one inch from the other fellow's nose.

When you come staggering home, cussing right and left and spewing and spitting, your wife suffers, your children suffer. Don't think that you are the only one that suffers. A man that goes to the penitentiary makes his wife and children suffer just as much as he does. You're placing a shame on your wife and children. If you're a dirty, low-down, filthy, drunken, whisky-soaked bum you'll affect all with whom you come in contact. If you're a God-fearing man you will influence all with whom you come in contact. You can't live by yourself.

I occasionally hear a man say, "It's nobody's business how I live." Then I say he is the most dirty, low-down, whisky-soaked, beer guzzling, bull-necked, foul-mouthed hypocrite that ever had a brain rotten enough to conceive such a statement and lips vile enough to utter it. You say, "If I am satisfied with my life why do you want to interfere with my business?"

If I heard a man beating his wife and heard her shrieks and the children's cries and my wife would tell me to go and see what was the matter, and I went in and found a great, big, broad-shouldered, whisky-soaked, hog-jowled, weasel-eyed brute dragging a little woman around by the hair, and two children in the corner unconscious from his kicks and the others yelling in abject terror, and he said, "What are you coming in to interfere with my personal liberty for? Isn't this my wife, didn't I pay for the license to wed her?" You ought, or you're a bigamist. "Aren't these children; didn't I pay the doctor to bring them into the world?" You ought to, or you're a thief. "If I want to beat them, what is that your business, aren't they mine?" Would I apologise? Never! I'd knock seven kinds of pork out of that old hog.

I remember when I was secretary of the Y.M.C.A. in Chicago, I had the saloon route. I had to go around and give tickets inviting men to come to the Y.M.C.A. services. And one day I was told to count the men going into a certain saloon. Not the ones already in, but just those going in. In sixty-two minutes I could count just 1,004 men going in there. I went in then and met a fellow who used to be my side-kicker out in Iowa, and he threw down a mint julep while I stood there, and I asked him what he was doing.

"Oh, just come down to the theater," he said, "and come over for a drink between acts."

"Why, you are three sheets in the wind now," I said, and then an old drunken bum, with a little threadbare coat, a straw hat, no vest, pants torn, toes sticking out through his torn shoes and several weeks' growth of beard on his face, came in and said to the bartender: "For God's sake, can't you give an old bum a drink of whisky to warm up on?" and the bartender poured him out a big glass and he gulped it down. He pulled his hat down and slouched out.

I said to my friend, "George, do you see that old drunken bum, down and out? There was a time when he was just like you. No drunkard ever intended to be a drunkard. Every drunkard intended to be a moderate drinker."

"Oh, you're unduly excited over my welfare," he said. "I never expect to get that far."

"Neither did that bum," I answered. I was standing on another corner less than eight months afterward and I saw a bum coming along with head down, his eyes bloodshot, his face bloated, and he panhandled me for a flapjack before I recognized him. It was George. He had lost his job and was on the toboggan slide hitting it for hell. I say if sin weren't so deceitful it wouldn't be so attractive. Every added drink makes it harder.

Some just live for booze. Some say, "I need it. It keeps me warm in winter." Another says, "It keeps me cool in summer." Well, if it keeps you warm in winter and cool in summer, why is it that out of those who freeze to death and are sun-struck the greater part of them are booze-hoisters? Every one takes it for the alcohol there is in it. Take that out and you would as soon as drink water.

I can buy a can of good beef extract and dip the point of my knife in the can and get more nourishment on the point of that knife than in 800 gallons of the best beer. If the brewers of this land today were making their beer in Germany, ninety per cent of them would be in jail. The extract on the point of the knife represents one and three-quarter pounds of good beefsteak. Just think, you have to make a swill barrel out of your bellies and a sewer if you want to get that much nourishment out of beer and run 800 gallons through. Oh, go ahead, if you want to, but I'll try to help you just the same.

Every man has blood corpuscles and their object is to take the impurities out of your system. Perspiration is impurities come out. Every time you work or I preach the impurities come out. Every time you sweat there is a destroying power going on inside. The blood goes through the heart every seventeen seconds. Oh, we have a marvelous system. In some spots there are 4,000 pores to the square inch and a grain of sand will cover 150 of them. I can strip you and cover you with shellac and you'll be dead in forty-eight hours. Oh, we are fearfully and wonderfully made.

Alcohol knocks the blood corpuscles out of business so that it takes eight to ten to do what one ought to do. There's a man who drinks. Here's a fellow who drives a beer wagon. Look how pussy he is. He's full of rotten tissue. He says he's healthy. Smell his breath. You punch your finger in that healthy flesh he talks about and the dent will be there a half hour afterwards. You look like you don't believe it. Try it when you go to bed tonight. Pneumonia has a first mortgage on a booze-hoister.

Take a fellow with good, healthy muscles, and you punch them and they bound out like a rubber band. The first thing about a crushed strawberry stomach is a crushed strawberry nose. Nature lets the public on the outside know what is going on inside. If I could just take the stomach of a moderate drinker and turn it wrong side out for you, it would be all the temperance lecture you would need. You know what alcohol does to the white of an egg. It will cook it in a few minutes. Well, alcohol does the same thing to the nerves as to the white of an egg. That's why some men can't walk. They stagger because their nerves are pretty paralyzed.

The liver is the largest organ of the body. It takes all of the blood in the body and purifies it and takes out the poisons and passes them on to the gall and from there they go to the intestines and act as oil does on machinery. When a man drinks the liver becomes covered with hob nails, and then refuses to work, and the poisons stay in the blood. Then the victim begins to turn yellow. He has the jaundice. The kidneys take what is left and purify that. The booze that a man drinks turns them hard.

That's what booze is doing for you. Isn't it time you went red hot after the enemy? I'm trying to help you. I'm trying to put a carpet on your floor, pull the pillows out of the windows, give you and your children and wife good clothes. I'm trying to get you to save your money instead of buying a machine for the saloon-keeper while you have to foot it.

By the grace of God I have strength enough to pass the open saloon, but some of you can't, so I owe it to you to help you.

I've stood for more sneers and scoffs and insults and had my life threatened from one end of the land to the other by this God-forsaken gang of thugs and cut-throats because I have come out uncompromisingly against them. I've taken more dirty, vile insults from this lowdown bunch than from any one on earth, but there is not one that will reach lower, or reach higher up or wider, to help you out of the pits of drunkenness than I.

The Unpardonable Sin

herefore I say unto you, All manner of sin and blasphemy shall be forgiven unto men: but the blasphemy against the Holy Ghost shall not be forgiven unto men. And whosoever speaketh a word against the Son of man, it shall be forgiven him: but whosoever speaketh against the Holy Ghost, it shall not be forgiven him, neither in this world, neither in the world to come."

I'd like to know where anybody ever found any authority for a belief in future probation. Jesus Christ was either human or he was divine. And if he was only human then I am not obligated to obey his word any more than I am that of any other philosopher.

The Pharisees charged Jesus with being in league with the devil. They said to him, "You have a devil." They grew bolder in their denunciation and said: "You do what you do through Beelzebub, the prince of devils." Jesus said: "How is that so? If what I do I do through the devil, explain why it is I am overthrowing the works of the devil. If I am a devil and if what I do is through the devil. I would not be doing what I am doing to destroy the works of the devil, but I would be working to destroy the works of God."

From that day forth they dared not ask him any questions.

I know there are various opinions held by men as to what they believe constitutes the sin against the Holy Ghost. There are those who think it could have been committed only by those who heard Jesus Christ speak and saw him in the flesh. If that be true then neither you nor I are in danger, for neither has ever seen Jesus in the flesh nor heard him. Another class think that it has been committed since the days of Jesus, but at extremely rare intervals; and still a third class think they have committed it and they spend their lives in gloom and dread and are perfectly useless to themselves and the community.

And yet I haven't the slightest doubt but that there are thousands that come under the head of my message, who are never gloomy, never depressed, never downcast; their conscience is at ease, their spirits are light and gay, they eat three meals a day and sleep as sound as a babe at night; nothing seems to disturb them, life is all pleasure and song.

If you will lay aside any preconceived ideas or opinions which you may have had or still have as to what you imagine, think or believe constitutes the sin against the Holy Ghost, or the unpardonable sin, and if you will listen to me, for I have read every sermon I could ever get my hands upon the subject, and have listened to every man I have ever had an opportunity to hear preach, and have read everything the Bible has taught on the subject.

I do not say that my views on the subject are infallible, but I have wept and prayed and studied over it, and if time will permit and my strength will allow and your patience endure, I will try and ask and answer a few questions. What is it? Why will God not forgive it?

It is not swearing. If swearing were the unpardonable sin, lots of men in heaven would have to go to hell and there are multitudes on earth on their way to heaven who would have to go to hell. It is not drunkenness. There are multitudes in heaven that have crept and crawled out of the quagmires of filth and the cesspools of iniquity and drunkenness. Some of the brightest lights that ever blazed for God have been men that God saved from drunkenness.

It's not adultery. Jesus said to the woman committing adultery and caught in the very act: "Neither do I condemn thee; go and sin no more."

It isn't theft. He said to Zaccheus, "This day is salvation come upon they house." Zaccheus had been a thief.

It's not murder. Men's hands have been red with blood and God has forgiven them. The Apostle Paul's hands were red with blood.

What is it? To me it is plain and simple. It is constant and continual, and final rejection of Jesus Christ as your Saviour. God's offer of mercy and salvation comes to you and you say, "No," and you push it aside. I do know that there is such a thing as the last call to every man or woman. God says that his spirit will not always strive with man, and when a man or woman says "No" as God's spirit strives for the last time it forever seals your doom.

It is no special form of sin, no one act. It might be swearing, it might be theft. Any one becomes unpardonable if God keeps calling on you to forsake that sin and you keep on refusing to forsake it, and if you don't then he will withdraw and let you alone and that sin will become unpardonable, for God won't ask you again to forsake it.

It is no one glaring act, but the constant repetition of the same thing. There will come a time when you commit that sin once too often.

It is a known law of mind that truth resisted loses its power on the mind that resists it. You hear a truth the first time and reject it. The next time the truth won't seem so strong and will be easier to resist. God throws a truth in your face. You reject it. He throws again; you reject again. Finally God will stop throwing the truth at you and you will have committed the unpardonable sin.

> "There is a line by us unseen;
>   It crosses every path;
> It is God's boundary between
>   His patience and his wrath.
>
> "To cross that limit is to die,
>   To die as if by stealth.
> It may not dim your eye,
>   Nor pale the glow of health,
>
> "Your conscience may be still at ease;
>   Your spirits light and gay;
> That which pleases still may please,
>   And care be thrown away;
>
> "But on that forehead God hath set
>   Indelibly a mark,
> Unseen by man; for man as yet
>   Is blind and in the dark.
>
> "Indeed, the doomed one's path below
>   May bloom as Edens bloom;
> He does not, will not know,
>   Nor believe that he is doomed."

Over in Scotland there are men who earn their living by gathering the eggs of birds, laid upon ledges on rocks away below the cliff top. They fasten a rope to a tree, also to themselves, then swing back and forth and in upon the ledge of rock. When a man was doing that same thing years ago, the rope beneath his arms became untied, and the protruding rock caused the rope to hang many feet beyond his reach.

The man waited for help to come, but none came. Darkness came, the light dawned, and he gave himself up to the fate of starvation, which he felt inevitably awaiting him, when a breeze freshened and the dangling rope began to vibrate. As the wind increased in velocity it increased the vibration of the rope and as it would bend in, he said: "If I miss it, I die; if I seize it, it's my only chance," and with a prayer to God as the rope bent in, he leaped out of the chasm and seized it and made his way hand over hand to the top, and when he reached it his hair was as white as the driven snow.

There is one cord that swings through this old world today—the Holy Spirit. With every invitation it swings farther away. We are living in the last dispensation, the dispensation of the Holy Spirit, and God is speaking to the world through the Holy Spirit today.

By every known law of the mind, conversion must be effected by the influence of the truth on the mind. Every time you resist the truth the next time you hear it, it loses its force on your mind. And every time you hear a truth and withstand it, then you become stronger in your power to resist 'the truth. We all know this, that each resistance strengthens you against the truth. When a man hears the truth and he resists it, the truth grows weaker and he grows stronger to resist it.

No matter what Jesus Christ did the Jews refused to believe. He had performed wonderful deeds but they wouldn't believe, so when Lazarus was dead, he said: "Lazarus, come forth," and then turned to the Jews and said: "Isn't that evidence enough that I am the Son of God?" and they cried: "Away with him." One day he was walking down the hot dusty road and he met a funeral procession. The mourners were bearing the body of a young man and his mother was weeping. He told them to place the coffin on the ground and said:

"Young man arise," and he arose. Then he asked the Pharisees: "Is that not proof enough that I am the Son of God, that I make the dead to arise?" and they cried: "Away with him." So no matter what Jesus did, the Jews refused to believe him. No matter what Jesus Christ says or does today, you'll refuse to accept, and continue to rush pell-mell to eternal damnation.

Jesus Christ gives you just as much evidence today. Down in Indiana, my friend, Mrs. Robinson, was preaching. I don't remember the town, but I think it was Kokomo, and I remember the incident, and the last day she tried to get the leader of society there to give her heart to God. She preached and then went down in the aisle and talked to her. Then she went back to the platform and made her appeal from there. Again she went to the girl, but she still refused. As Mrs. Robinson turned to go she saw her borrow a pencil from her escort and write something in the back of a hymn book.

A few years afterward Mrs. Robinson went back to the town and was told the girl was dying. They told her the physicians had just held a consultation and said she could not live until night. Mrs. Robinson hurried to her home. The girl looked up, recognized her and said: "I didn't send for you. You came on your own account, and you're too late." To every appeal she would reply: "You're too late." Finally she said: "Go look in the hymn book in the church."

They hurried to the church and looked over the hymn books and found in the back of one her name and address and these words, "I'll run the risk; I'll take my chance." That was the last call to her. Not any one sin is the unpardonable sin, but it may be that constant repetition, over and over again until God will say: "Take it and go to hell."

Who can commit it? I used to think that only the vile, the profane were the people who could commit it.

Whom did Jesus warn? The Pharisees. And who were they? The best men, morally, in Jerusalem.

Who can commit it? Any man or woman who says "No" to Jesus Christ. You may even defend the Bible. You may be the best man or woman, morally, in the world. Your name may be synonymous with virtue and purity, but let God try to get into your heart, let him try to get you to walk down the aisle and publicly acknowledge Jesus Christ, and your heart and lips are sealed like a bank vault, and God hasn't been able to pull you to your feet. And God won't keep on begging you to do it.

Something may say to you, "I ought to be a Christian." This is the dispensation of the Holy Spirit. God spoke in three dispensations. First, through the old Mosaic law. Then Jesus Christ came upon this earth and lived and the Jews and Gentiles conspired to kill him. Then the Holy Spirit came down at Pentecost and God is speaking through the Holy Spirit today. The Holy Spirit is pressing you to be a Christian. It takes the combined efforts to the Trinity to keep you out of hell—God the Father to provide the plan of salvation, the Holy Spirit to convict, Jesus Christ to redeem you through his blood, and your acceptance and repentance to save you. Sin is no trifle.

The only representative of the Trinity in the world today is the Holy Ghost. Jesus has been here, but he is not here now—that is, in flesh and blood. The Holy Ghost is here now. When he leaves the world, good-bye.

There was an old saint of God, now in glory. He was holding meetings one time and a young man came down the aisle and went so far as to ask him to pray for him. He said: "Let's settle it now," but the young man refused and told him to pray for him. Years afterwards, in Philadelphia, the old saint was in a hotel waiting for his card to be taken up to the man he wanted to see. He looked in the bar-room door. There was a young man ordering a drink. The two saw each other's reflections in the French plate behind the bar, and the young man came out and said: "How do you do?" The old man spoke to him.

The young fellow said: "I suppose you don't remember me?" and the old saint had to admit that he did not.

The young fellow asked him if he remembered the meeting eleven years before in New York when a young man came down the aisle and asked him to pray for him. He said he was the young man. The old saint said: "From what I have just seen I would suppose that you did not settle it."

The young fellow said: "I did not and I never expect to. I believe there is a hell and I'm going there as fast as I can go."

The old man begged him to keep still, but he said: "It is true. If Jesus Christ would come through that door now I would spit in his face."

The old man said: "Don't talk that way. I would not stand to have you talk about my wife that way, and I will not stand it to have you talk about Christ that way." The young fellow said it was all true. The old fellow said: "Maybe it is all true, but I do not like to hear it." The young fellow said it was true, and that if he had a Bible he would tear it up. With a string of oaths he went to the bar, took two or three drinks and went out the door.

Sometimes it may be utter, absolute indifference. Some can hear any sermon and any song and not be moved. I'll venture that some of you have not been convicted of sin for twenty-five years. Back yonder the Spirit of God convicted you and you didn't yield. The first place I ever preached, in the little town of Garner, in Hancock county, Iowa, a man came down the aisle. I said, "Who's that?" and someone told me that he was one of the richest men in the county. I asked him what I had said to help him, and he said nothing. Then he told me that twenty-one years ago he had gone to Chicago and sold his stock four hours before he had to catch a train. Moody was in town and with a friend he had gone and stood inside the door, listening to the sermon. When Moody gave the invitation he handed his coat and hat to his friend and said he was going down to give Moody his hand. The friend told him not to do it, that he would miss his train, and then the railroad pass would be no good after that day. He said he could afford to pay his way home.

His friend told him not to go up there amid all the excitement, but to wait and settle it at home. He said he had waited thirty-five years and hadn't settled it at home, but the friend persisted against his going forward and giving his heart to God. Finally the time passed and they had to catch the train and the man hadn't gone forward. He told me that he had never had a desire to give his heart to God until that time, twenty-one years later, when he heard me preach. The Spirit called him when he heard Moody, and then the Spirit did not call him again until twenty-one years later, when he heard me.

I have never said and I never will say that all unbelievers died in agony. Man ordinarily dies as he has lived. If you have lived in unbelief, ninety-nine cases out of one hundred you'll die that way. If Christianity is a good thing to die with it is a good thing to live with.

I don't go much on these death-bed confessions. A death-bed confession is like burning a candle at both ends and then blowing the smoke in the face of Jesus. A death-bed confession is like drinking the cup of life and then offering the dregs to Christ. I think it is one of the most contemptible, miserable, low-down, unmanly and unwomanly things that you can do, to keep your life in your own control until the last moment and then try to creep into the kingdom on account of the long-suffering and mercy of Jesus Christ. I don't say that none is genuine. But there is only one on record in the Bible, and that was the first time the dying thief had ever heard of Christ, and he accepted at once. So your case is not analogous to this. You have wagon loads of sermons dumped into you, but it's a mighty hard thing to accept in the last moment. If you've lived without conviction, your friends ought not to get mad when the preacher preaches your funeral sermon, if he doesn't put you in the front row in heaven, with a harp in your hands and a crown on your head.

God can forgive sins but you have got to comply with his requirements. He is not willing that any shall perish, but he has a right to tell me and you what to do to be saved.

A doctor had been a practitioner for sixty years and he was asked how many Godless men he had seen show any trace of concern on their death-bed. He said he had kept track of three hundred and only three had shown any real concern. That is appalling to me. You ordinarily die as you have lived.

A minister was called to a house of shame to be with a dying girl in her last moments. He prayed and then looked at her face and saw no signs of hope of repentance. He was led to pray again and this time he was led to put in a verse of scripture, Isaiah 1:18: "Come now and let us reason together, saith the Lord: Though your sins be as scarlet, they shall be as white as now; though they be red like crimson, they shall be as wool."

"Would you pray again and put in that verse?" the girl asked and as he started she called, "Stop! Let me put my finger on that verse." The minister prayed and when he looked again, he saw hope and pardon and peace in the girl's face. "I'm so glad God made that 'scarlet,'" she said, "for that means me."

All manner of sins God will forgive. Then tell me why you will not come when God says, "All manner of sin and blasphemy shall be forgiven unto men." Great heavens! I can't understand how you sit still.

But a man says: "Bill, will He forgive a murderer? My hands are red with blood, although no one knows it." Didn't I say he forgave Paul?

A friend of mine was preaching in Lansing, Michigan, one time and in the middle section of the church there was a man who made him so nervous he couldn't watch him and preach. Nothing seemed to attract him until he said, "Supposing there were a murderer here tonight, God would forgive him if he accepted Christ," and the man grabbed the chair in front of him at the word murderer and sat rigid throughout the sermon, never taking his eyes from my friend. At the end of the meeting my friend went down to him and asked him what was the matter, telling him that he had made him so nervous he could hardly preach. The man said: "I'm a murderer. I escaped through a technicality and I'm supporting the widow and children, but I am a murderer." My friend brought him to Jesus Christ and now that man is a power in the Church. All manner of sins God says he will forgive.

Some say: "Mr. Sunday, why is it that so few aged sinners are converts?"

Infidels when asked this, seize upon it as a plan of attack. When God begins to show his power, then the devil and all of the demons of hell get busy. That's the best evidence in the world that these meetings are doing good, when that bunch of knockers gets busy. Infidels sneer and say: "How does it happen that when a man's mind has developed through age and experience and contact with the world, and he has passed the period of youthful enthusiasm, how does it happen that so few of them are converted?"

Religion makes its appeal to your sensibility, not to your intellect. The way into the kingdom of heaven is heart first, not head first. God is not an explanation; God is a revelation.

A grain of corn is a revelation, but you can't explain it. You know that if you put the vegetable kingdom in the mineral kingdom the vegetable will be born again, but you can't explain it. Some of the greatest things are revelations. Therefore, instead of being an argument against religion, it is an argument for it.

Don't you know that sixteen out of twenty who are converted are converted before they are twenty years old? Don't you know that eighteen out of thirty who are converted are converted before they are thirty years old? Don't you know that?

What does that prove? It proves that if you are not converted before you are thirty years old the chances are about 100,000 to one that you never will be converted.

Most people are converted at special revival services. I want to hurl this in the teeth, cram it down the throats of those who sneer at revival efforts—preachers included. Almost nine-tenths of the Christians at this meeting were converted at a revival. What does that show? It shows that if you are thirty and have not been converted, the chances are that if you are not converted at this revival you never will be converted.

If it weren't for revivals, just think of what hell would be like. Then think of any low-down, God-forsaken, dirty gang knocking a revival.

God says: "You can spurn my love and trample the blood under your feet, but if you seek my pardon I will forgive you." You might have been indifferent to the appeals of the minister, you might have been a thief, or an adulterer, or a blasphemer, or a scoffer, and all that, but God says: "I will forgive you." You might have been indifferent to the tears of poor wife and children and friends, but if you will seek God he will forgive you.

But when He came down and revealed himself as the Son of God through the Holy Spirit, if you sneer and say it is not true, your sin may become unpardonable. If you don't settle it here you never will settle it anywhere else.

I will close with a word of comfort and a word of warning. If you have a desire to be a Christian it is proof that the devil hasn't got you yet. That is the comfort. Now for the warning: If you have that desire thank God for it and yield to it. You may never have another chance.

A Plain Talk to Men

ejoice, O young man, in thy youth; and yet thy heart cheer thee in the days of thy youth, and walk in the ways of thine heart, and in the sight of thine eyes: but know thou that for all these things God will bring thee into judgment. Be not deceived; God is not mocked; for whatsoever a man soweth that shall he also reap.

In other words, do just as you please; lie if you want to, steal if you want to. God won't stop you, but he will hold you responsible in the end. Do just as you please until the end comes and the undertaker comes along and pumps the embalming fluid into you and then you are all in.

No one is living in ignorance of what will become of him if he does not go right and trot square. He knows there is a heaven for the saved and a hell for the damned, and that's all there is to it.

Many men start out on a life of pleasure. Please remember two things. First, pleasure soon has an end, and, second, there is a day of judgment coming and you'll get what's coming to you. God gives every man a square deal.

If a man stood up and told me he was going to preach on the things I am this afternoon, I'd want him to answer me several questions, and if he could do that I'd tell him to go ahead.

First—Are you kindly disposed toward me!
Second—Are you doing this to help me?
Third—Do you know what you're talking about?
Fourth—Do you practice what you preach?

That's fair. Well, for the first. God knows I am kindly disposed toward you. Second, God knows I would do anything in my power to help you be a better man. I want to make it easier for you to be square, and harder for you to go to hell. Third, I know what I'm talking about, for I have the Bible to back me up in parts and the statements of eminent physicians in other parts. And fourth, "Do I practice what I preach?" I will defy and challenge any man or woman on earth, and I'll look any man in the eye and challenge him, in the twenty-seven years I have been a professing Christian, to show anything against me. If I don't live what I preach, gentlemen, I'll leave the pulpit and never walk back here again. I live as I preach and I defy the dirty dogs who have insulted me and my wife and spread black-hearted lies and vilifications.

I was born and bred on a farm and at the age of eleven I held my place with men in the harvest field. When I was only nine years old I milked ten cows every morning. I know what hard knocks are. I have seen the seamy side of life. I have crawled out of the sewers and squalor and want. I have struggled ever since I was six years old, an orphan son of a dead soldier, up to this pulpit this afternoon. I know what it is to go to bed with an honest dollar in my overalls pocket, when the Goddess of Liberty became a Jenny Lind and the eagle on the other side became a nightingale and they'd sing a poor, homeless orphan boy to sleep. I'm not here to explode hot air and theories to you.

Some men here in town, if their wives asked them if they were coming down here, would say: "Oh no, I don't want to go anywhere I can't take you, dear." The dirty old dogs, they've been many a place they wouldn't take their wife and they wouldn't even let her know they were there.

If sin weren't so deceitful it wouldn't be so attractive. The effects get stronger and stronger while you get weaker and weaker all the time, and there is less chance of breaking away.

Many think a Christian has to be a sort of dish-rag proposition, a wishy-washy, sissified sort of a galoot that lets everybody make a doormat out of him. Let me tell you the manliest man is the man who will acknowledge Jesus Christ.

Christianity is the capital on which you build your character. Don't you let the devil fool you. You never become a man until you become a Christian. Christianity is the capital on which you do business. It's your character that gets you anything. Your reputation is what people say about you, but your character is what God and your wife and the angels know about you. Many have reputations of being good, but their

It is difficult to interpret William Ashley Sunday's impact on an era that had for its heroes Charles Lindbergh, Babe Ruth, Charlie Chaplin, Ernest Hemingway, Jimmy Walker. Certainly he shared their ebullience and individuality. And by combining a keen instinct for personal publicity with the tenets of religious fundamentalism, he became the nation's most popular "force for good" during the tumultuous Jazz Age.

Billy met his future wife, Helen A. Thompson (right), while playing for the Chicago White Stockings. After a courtship of five years, the couple married in 1888. A former Sunday school teacher, Miss Thompson made a perfect match for the evangelist, who became tremendously despondent whenever his calling forced them to be apart.

As spectacular on the stump as on the diamond, the whirling dervish called Billy Sunday struck as much fear into the faithful as did the "divil" himself. The years did not seem to have any appreciable effect on his style—on the left he is 38, on the right a supple 61.

PHOTOWORLD

CULVER PICTURES

In the Twenties, film luminaries recognized in Billy Sunday a kinship of spirit. At far left, Cecil B. DeMille smiles wryly at the evangelist over reigning star Mary Pickford. Billy's family is on his left.

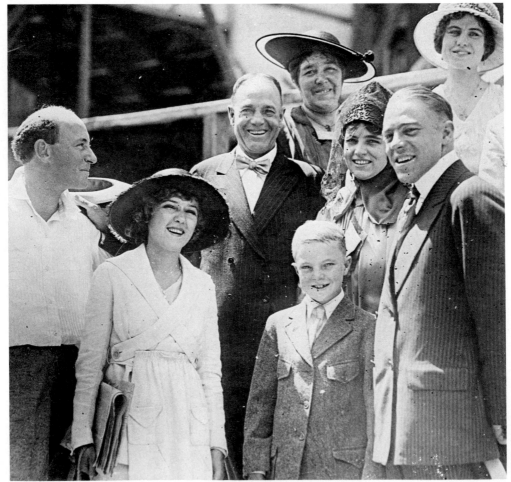

Billy could empty a bottle of "booze" with the best of the Drys. But while crusading against the evils of the flesh, he welcomed meeting Mae West, the national symbol of sex and sin.

Crowds in the tens of thousands often assembled to get religion from Billy. At left, a Paterson, New Jersey throng awaits the evangelist. Below, he speaks at the Calvary Baptist Church in New York City a year before his death.

characters would make a black mark on a piece of coal or tarred paper.

I was over in Terre Haute, Indiana, not long ago, and I was in a bank there admiring the beauty of it when the vice-president, Mr. McCormick, a friend of mine, said: "Bill, you haven't seen the vault yet," and he opened up the vaults there, carefully contrived against burglars, and let me in. There were three, and I wandered from one to another. No one watched me. I could have filled my pockets with gold or silver, but no one watched me. Why did they trust me? Because they knew I was preaching the gospel of Jesus Christ, and living up to it. That's why they trusted me. There was a time in my life when a man wouldn't trust me with a yellow dog on a corner fifteen minutes.

Before I was converted I could go five rounds so fast you couldn't see me for the dust, and I'm still pretty handy with my dukes and I can still deliver the goods with all express charges prepaid. Before I was converted I could run one hundred yards in ten seconds and circle the bases in fourteen seconds, and I could run just as fast after I was converted. So you don't have to be a dish-rag proposition at all.

When a person's acts affect only himself they can be left to the conscience of the individual, but when they affect others the law steps in. When a child has diphtheria, you are not allowed personal liberty; you are quarantined, because your personal liberty could endanger others if exercised. So you haven't any right to live in sin. You say you'll do it anyhow. All right, you'll go to hell, too. Adam and Eve said they would eat the apple anyhow, and the world became a graveyard, and here's the result today.

I look out into the world and see a man living in sin, I argue with him, I plead with him. I cry out warning words. I brand that man with a black brand, whose iniquities are responsible for the fall of others.

No man lives to himself alone. I hurt or help others by my life. When you go to hell you're going to drag some one else down with you and if you go to heaven you're going to take some one else with you. You say you hate sin. Of course you do if you have self-respect. But you never saw anyone who hates sin worse than I do, or loves a sinner more than I. I'm fighting for the sinners. I'm fighting to save your soul, just as a doctor fights to save your life from a disease. I'm your friend, and you'll find that I'll not compromise one bit with sin. I'll do anything to help you. No man will argue that sin is a good thing. Not a one who does not believe that the community would be better off if there was no sin. I preach against vice to show you that it will make your girl an outcast and your boy a drunkard. I'm fighting everything that will lead to this and if I have to be your enemy to fight it, God pity you, for I'm going to fight. People do not fight sin until it becomes a vice.

You say you're not afraid of sin. You ought to be, for your children. It doesn't take boys long to get on the wrong track, and while you are scratching gravel to make one lap, your boy makes ten. We've got kids who have not yet sprouted long breeches who know more about sin and vice than Methuselah. There are little frizzled-top sissies not yet sprouting long dresses who know more about vice than did their great-grandmothers when they were seventy-five years old. The girl who drinks will abandon her virtue. What did Methuselah know about smoking cigarettes? I know there are some sissy fellows out there who object to my talking plain and know you shirk from talking plain.

If any one ever tells you that you can't be virtuous and enjoy good health, I brand him as a low, infamous, blackhearted liar.

Ask any afflicted man you see on the street. If you could only reveal the heart of every one of them! In most you would find despair and disease.

How little he thinks when he is nursing that lust that he is nursing a demon which, like a vampire, will suck his blood and wreck his life and blacken and blight his existence. And if any little children are born to him, they will be weak anemics without the proper blood in their veins to support them. Our young men ought to be taught that no sum they can leave to a charitable institution can blot out the deeds of an ignominious life. You don't have to look far for the reason why so many young men fail; why they go through life weak, ambitionless, useless.

Let's be common folks together today. Let's be men, and talk sense.

As a rule a man wants something better for his children than he has had for himself. My father died before I was born and I lived with my grandfather. He smoked, but he didn't want me to. He chewed, but he didn't want me to. He drank, but he didn't want me to. He cussed, but he didn't want me to. He made wine that would make a man fight his own mother after he had drunk it. I remember how I used to find the bottles and suck the wine through a straw or an onion top.

One day a neighbor was in and my grandfather asked him for a chew. He went to hand it back, and I wanted some. He said I couldn't have it. I said I wanted it anyhow, and he picked me up and turned me across his knee and gave me a crack that made me see stars as big as moons.

If there is a father that hits the booze, he doesn't want his son to. If he is keeping some one on the side, he doesn't want his son to. In other words, you would not want your son to live like you if you are not living right.

An old general was at the bedside of his dying daughter. He didn't believe in the Bible and his daughter said, "What shall I do? You don't believe in the Bible. Mamma does. If I obey one I'm going against the other." The old general put his arms around his daughter and said: "Follow your mother's way; it is the safest." Man wants his children to have that which is sure.

I have sometimes imagined that young fellow in Luke XV. He came to his father and said, "Dig up. I'm tired of this and want to see the world." His father didn't know what he meant. "Come across with the mazuma, come clean, divvy. I want the coin, see?" Finally the father tumbled, and he said, "I got you," and he divided up his share and gave it to the young man. Then he goes down to Babylon and starts out on a sporting life. He meets the young blood and the gay dame. I can imagine that young fellow the first time he swore. If his mother had been near he would have looked at her and blushed rose red. But he thought he had to cuss to be a man.

No man can be a good husband, no man can be a good father, no man can be a respectable citizen, no man can be a gentleman, and swear. You can hang out a sign of gentleman, but when you cuss you might as well take it in.

There are three things which will ruin any town and give it a bad name—open licensed saloons; a dirty, cussing, swearing gang of black-legs on the street; and vile story tellers. Let a town be known for these three things, and these alone, and you could never start a boom half big enough to get one man there.

Old men, young men, boys, swear. What do you cuss for? It doesn't do you any good, gains you nothing in business or society; it loses you the esteem of men. God said more about cussing than anything. God said, "Thou shalt not kill," "Thou shalt not steal," "Thou shalt not bear false witness," but God said more about cussing than them all; and men are still cussing. "Thou shalt not take the name of the Lord thy God in vain, for the Lord will not hold him guiltless who taketh his name in vain."

I can see how you can get out of anything but cussing. I can see how a man could be placed in such a position that he would kill and be exonerated by the law of God and man, if he killed to protect his life, or the life of another.

I can see how a man could be forced to steal if he stole to keep his wife from starving.

Up in Chicago several years ago there was a long-continued strike and the last division of the union treasury had given each man twenty-five cents. A man went into the railroad yards and got a bag of coal from one of the cars. They pinched him and he came up before a judge. He told the judge that he had only the twenty-five cents of the last division and he spent that for food. His wife and two children were at home starving and he had no fire. He stole the coal to cook their food. The judge thundered, "Get out of this room and get home and build that fire as quickly as you can."

Say, boys, if I was on a jury and you could prove to me that a father had stolen a loaf of bread to keep his wife from starving you could keep me in the room until the ants took me out through the keyhole before I'd stick him. That may not be law, I don't know; but you'll find there is a big streak of human nature in Bill.

There isn't a fellow in this crowd but what would be disgusted if his wife or sister would cuss and hit the booze like he does. If she would put fifteen or twenty beers under her belt, he'd go whining around a divorce court for a divorce right away and say he couldn't live with her. Why, you dirty dog, she has to live with you.

I heard of a fellow whose wife thought she would show him how he sounded around the house and give him a dose of his own medicine. So one morning he came down and asked for his breakfast. "Why you old blankety, blank, blank, bald-headed, blankety, blankety, blank, you can get your own breakfast." He was horrified, but every time he tried to say anything she would bring out a bunch of lurid oaths until finally he said "Wife, if you'll cut out that cussing I'll never swear again."

I have sometimes tried to imagine myself in Damascus on review day, and have seen a man riding on a horse richly caparisoned with trappings of gold and silver, and he himself clothed in garments of the finest fabrics, and the most costly, though with a face so sad and melancholy that it would cause the beholder to turn and look a second and third time. But he was a leper. And a man unaccustomed to such scenes might be heard to make a remark like this: "How unequally God seems to divide his favors! There is a man who rides and others walk; he is clothed in costly garments; they are almost naked while he is well fed," and they contrast the difference between the man on the horse and the others. If we only knew the breaking hearts of the people we envy we would pity them from the bottom of our souls.

I was being driven through a suburb of Chicago by a real estate man who wanted to sell me a lot. He was telling me who lived here and who lived there, and what an honor it would be for me and my children to possess a home there. We were driving past a house that must have cost $100,000 and he said: "That house is owned by Mr. So-and-So. He is one of our multi-millionaires, and he and his wife have been known to live in that house for months and never speak to each other. They each have separate apartments, each has a separate retinue of servants, each a dining-room and sleeping apartments, and months come and go by and they never speak to each other." My thoughts hurried back to the little flat we called our home, where we had lived for seventeen years. I have paid rent enough to pay for it. There wasn't much in it; I could load it in two furniture vans, maybe three, counting the piano, but I would not trade the happiness and the joy and the love of that little flat if I had to take that palatial home and the sorrow and the things that went with it.

Suppose you were driving along the street and a man who was intimately acquainted with the skeletons that are in every family, should tell you the secrets of them all, of that boy who has broken his father's heart by being a drunkard, a black-leg gambler, and that girl who has gone astray, and that wife who is a common drunkard, made so by society, and the father himself who is also a sinner.

Leprosy is exceedingly loathsome, and as I study its pathology I am not surprised that God used it as a type of sin. A man who is able to understand this disease, its beginning and its progress, might be approached by a man who was thus afflicted and might say to him, "Hurry! hurry! Show yourself to the priest for the cleansing of the Mosaic law."

"Why?" says the man addressed. "What is the trouble?" The other man would say, "Do hurry and show yourself to the priest." But the man says, "That is only a fester, only a water blister, only a pimple, nothing more. I say there is no occasion to be alarmed. You are unduly agitated and excited for my welfare."

Those sores are only few now, but it spreads, and it is first upon the hand, then upon the arm, and from the arm it goes on until it lays hold of every nerve, artery, vein with its slimy coil, and continues until the disintegration of the parts takes place and they drop off, and then it is too late. But the man who was concerned saw the beginning of that, not only the end, but the beginning. He looked yonder and saw the end too. If you saw a blaze you would cry, "Fire!" Why? Because you know that if let alone it will consume the building.

That is the reason why you hurry when you get evidence of the disease. So I say to you, young man, don't you go with that godless, good-for-nothing gang that blaspheme and sneer at religion, that bunch of character assassins; they will make of your body a doormat to wipe their feet upon. Don't go with that bunch. I heard you swear, I heard you sneer at religion. Stop, or you will become a staggering, muttering, bleary-eyed, foul-mouthed down-and-outer, on your way to hell. I say to you stop, or you will go reeling down to hell, breaking your wife's heart and wrecking your children's lives. And what have you got to show for it? What have you got to show for it? God pity you for all you got to show for selling your soul to the devil. You are a fool. You are a fool. Take it from "Bill," you are a fool.

Don't you go, my boy; don't you laugh at that smutty story with a double meaning. Don't go with that gang. But you say to me, "Mr. Sunday, you are unduly excited for my welfare. I know you smell liquor on my breath, but I never expect to become a drunkard. I never expect to become an outcast." Well, you are a fool. You are a fool. No man ever intended to become a drunkard. Every drunkard started out to be simply a moderate drinker. The fellow that tells me that he can leave it alone when he wants to lies. It is a lie. If you can, why don't you leave it alone? You will never let it alone. If you could, you would. My boy, hear me, I have walked along the shores of time, and have seen them strewn with the wrecks of those who have drifted in from the seas of lust and passion and are fit only for danger signals to warn the coming race. You can't leave it alone or if you can, the time will come when it will get you. Take it from me.

My mother told me never to buy calico by lamplight, because you can't tell whether the colors will stand or run in the wash. Never ask a girl to be your wife when she's got her best bib and tucker on. Call on her and leave at ten o'clock and leave your glove on the piano, and go back the next morning about nine o'clock after your glove and ring the doorbell, and if she comes to the door with her hair done up in curl papers and a slipper on one foot and a shoe on the other foot, and that untied, and a Mother Hubbard on, take to the woods as fast as you can go. Never mind the glove, let the old man have that if he can wear it. But if she comes to the door nice and neat in a neat working house dress, with her sleeves rolled up and her hair neatly done up, and a ribbon or a flower stuck in it, grab her quick.

Henry Clay Trumbull told me years ago that he was in Europe and in London he went to a theater to see a man who was going to give an exhibition of wild animals and serpents. He had a royal Bengal tiger and a Numidian lion, and he introduced a beast that seems to be least able of being tamed either by kindness or brutality, a black panther. He made him go through the various motions, and after a while a wire screen was put down in front of the stage between the audience and the performer, and to the weird strains of an oriental band the man approached from the left of the stage and a serpent from the right. The eyes of the serpent and the man met and the serpent quailed before the man. Man was master there. At his command the serpent went through various contortions, and the man stepped to the front of the stage and the serpent wound himself round and round and round the man, until the man and serpent seemed as one. His tongue shot out, his eyes dilated. The man gave a call, but the audience thought that part of the performance, and that horrified audience sat there and heard bone after bone in that man's body crack and break as the reptile tightened its grasp upon his body, and saw his body crushed before he could be saved.

He had bought that snake when it was only four feet long and he had watered and nursed it until it was thirty-five feet. At first he could have killed it; at last it killed him.

Are you nursing a habit today? Is it drink? Are you nursing and feeding that which will wreck your life and wreck you upon the shores of passion, notwithstanding all the wrecks you have seen of those who have gone down the line?

I never got such a good idea of leprosy as I did by reading that wonderful book of the nineteenth century by General Lew Wallace, "Ben Hur." You remember the banishment of Ben Hur and the disintegration of that family life and estate, and the return of Ben Hur from his exile. He goes past his old home. The blinds are closed and drawn and all is deserted. He lies down upon the door-step and falls asleep. His mother and sister have been in the leper colony and are dying of leprosy and only waiting the time when they will be covered with the remains of others who have come there. So they have come to the city to get bread and secure water, and they see their son and brother lying on the door-step of their old home. They dare not awaken him for fear anguish at learning of their fate would be more than he could bear. They dare not touch him because it is against the law, so they creep close to him and put their leprous lips against his sandal-covered feet. They then go back again with the bread and water for which they had come.

Presently Ben Hur awakens and rubs his eyes and sees great excitement. (This part of the story is mine.) Along comes a blear-eyed, old, whisky-soaked degenerate and Ben Hur asks him what is the trouble, what is the excitement about, and he says: "A couple of lepers have been cleansed, but there is nothing to that, just some occult power, it's all a fake." Ben Hur goes farther on and hears about this wonder, and they say it is nothing; nothing, some long-haired evangelist who says his name is Jesus Christ; it's all a fake. Then Ben Hur goes farther and discovers that it is Jesus of Nazareth and that he has cleansed Ben Hur's own mother and sister. He hears the story and acknowledges the Nazarene.

The lepers had to cry, "Unclean! Unclean!" in those days to warn the people. They were compelled by law to do that: also they were compelled by law to go on the side of the street toward which the wind was blowing lest the breeze bring the germs of their body to the clean and infect them with the disease. And the victim of this disease was compelled to live in a lonely part of the city, waiting until his teeth began to drop out, his eyes to drop from their sockets, and his fingers to drop from his hands, then he was compelled to go out in the tombs, the dying among the dead, there to live until at last he was gathered to the remains of the dead. That was the law that governed the leper in those days. All others shrank from him; he went forth alone. Alone! No man of all he loved or knew, was with him; he went forth on his way, alone, sick at heart, to die alone.

Leprosy is infectious. And so is sin. Sin begins in so-called innocent flirtation. The old, god-forsaken scoundrel of a libertine, who looks upon every woman as legitimate prey for his lust, will contaminate a community; one drunkard, staggering and maundering and muttering his way down to perdition, will debauch a town.

Some men ought to be hurled out of society; they ought to be kicked out of lodges; they ought to be kicked out of churches, and out of politics, and every other place where decent men live or associate. And I want to lift the burden tonight from the heads of the unoffending womanhood and hurl it on the heads of offending manhood.

Rid the world of those despicable beasts who live off the earnings of the unfortunate girl who is merchandising herself for gain. In some sections they make a business of it. I say commercialized vice is hell. I do not believe any more in a segregated district for immoral women than I would in having a section for thieves to live in where you could hire one any day or night in the week to steal for you. There are two things which have got to be driven out or they'll drive us out, and they are open licensed saloons and protected vice.

Society needs a new division of anathemas. You hurl the burden on the head of the girl; and the double-dyed scoundrel that caused her ruin is received in society with open arms, while the girl is left to hang her head and spend her life in shame. Some men are so rotten and vile that they ought to be disinfected and take a bath in carbolic acid and formaldehyde. Shut the lodge door in the face of every man that you know to be a moral leper; don't let him hide behind his uniform and his badge when you know him to be so rotten that the devil would duck up an alley rather than meet him face to face. Kick him out of church. Kick him out of society.

You don't live your life alone. Your life affects others. Some girls will walk the streets and pick up every Tom, Dick and Harry that will come across with the price of an ice-cream soda or a joy ride.

So with the boy. He will sit at your table and drink beer, and I want to tell you if you are low-down enough to serve beer and wine in your home, when you serve it you are as low down as the saloon-keeper, and I don't care whether you do it for society or for anything else. If you serve liquor or drink you are as low down as the saloon-keeper in my opinion. So the boy who had not grit enough to turn down his glass at the banquet and refuse to drink is now a blear-eyed, staggering drunkard, reeling to hell. He couldn't stand the sneers of the crowd. Many a fellow started out to play cards for beans, and tonight he would stake his soul for a show-down. The hole in the gambling table is not very big; it is about big enough to shove a dollar through; but it is big enough to shove your wife through; big enough to shove your happiness through; your home through; your salary, your character; just big enough to shove everything that is dear to you in this world through.

Listen to me. Bad as it is to be afflicted with physical leprosy, moral leprosy is ten thousand times worse. I don't care if you are the richest man in the town, the biggest taxpayer in the county, the biggest politician in the district, or in the state. I don't care a rap if you carry the political vote of Pennsylvania in your vest pocket, and if you can change the vote from Democratic to Republican in the convention—if after your worldly career is closed my text would make you a fitting epitaph for your tombstone and obituary notice in the papers, then what difference would it make what you had done—"he was a leper." He was a great politician—but "He was a leper." What difference would it make?

I'll tell you, I was never more interested in my life than in reading the story of an old Confederate colonel who was a stickler for martial discipline. One day he had a trifling case of insubordination. He ordered his men to halt, and he had the offender shot. They dug the grave and he gave the command to march, and they had stopped just three minutes by the clock. At the close of the war they made him chief of police of a Southern city, and he was so vile and corrupt that the people arose and ordered his dismissal. Then a great earthquake swept over the city, and the people rushed from their homes and thousands of people crowded the streets and there was great excitement. Some asked, "Where is the colonel?" and they said, "You will find him in one of two or three places." So they searched and found him in a den of infamy. He was so drunk that he didn't realize the danger he was in. They led him out, then put him upon a snow white-horse, put his spurs on his boots and his regimentals on; they pinned a star on his breast and put a cockade on his hat, and said to him: "Colonel, we command you as mayor of the city to quell this riot. You have supreme authority."

He rode out among the people to quell the riot, dug his spurs into the white side of the horse and the crimson flowed out, and he rode in and out among the surging mass of humanity.

He rode out among the people with commands here, torrents of obscenity there, and in twenty-five minutes the stillness of death reigned in city squares, so marvelously did they fear him, so wonderful was his power over men. He then rode out, dismounted, took off his cockade, tore the star from his breast and threw it down, threw off his regimentals, took off his sword; then he staggered back to the house of infamy, where three months later he died, away from his wife, away from virtue, away from morality, his name synonymous with all that is vile. What difference did it make that he had power over men when you might sum up his life in the words, "But he was a leper." What difference did it make?

I pity the boy or girl from the depths of my soul, who if you ask are you willing to be a Christian, will answer: "Mr. Sunday, I would like to be, but if I tell that at home my brothers will abuse me, my mother will sneer at me, my father will curse me. If I were, I would have no encouragement to stand and fight the battle." I pity from the depths of my soul that boy or girl, the boy who has a father like that; the girl that has a mother like that, who have a joint like that for a home.

Unclean! Suppose every young man who is a moral leper were impelled by some uncontrollable impulse over which he had no power to make public revelations of his sins! Down the street he comes in his auto and you speak to him from the curbstone and he will say: "Unclean! Unclean!" Yonder he comes walking down the street. Suppose that to every man and woman he meets he is impelled and compelled to make revelation of the fact that he is a leper.

Leprosy is an infectious disease; it is the germ of sin. If there is an evil in you the evil will dwell in others. When we do wrong we inspire others—and your lives scatter disease when you come in contact with others. If there is sin in the father there will be sin in the boy; if there is sin in the mother, there will be sin in the daughter; if there is sin in the sister, there will be sin in the brother; by your influence you will spread it. If you live the wrong way you will drag somebody else to perdition with you as you go, and kindred ties will facilitate it.

Supposing all your hearts were open. Supposing we had glass doors to our hearts, and we could walk down the street and look in and see where you have been, and with whom you have been and what you have been doing. A good many of you would want stained-glass windows and heavy tapestry to cover them.

Suppose I could put a screen behind me, pull a string or push a button, and produce on that screen a view of the hearts of the people. I would say: "Here is Mr. and Mrs. A's life, as it is, and here, as the people think it is. Here is what he really is. Here is where he has been. Here is how much booze he drinks. Here is how much he lost last year at horse races." But these are the things that society does not take note of. Society takes no note of the flirtation on the street. It waits until the girl has lost her virtue and then it slams the door in her face. It takes no note of that young man drinking at a banquet table; it waits until he becomes a bleary-eyed drunkard and then it will slam the door in his face. It will take no note of the young fellow that plays cards for a prize; it waits until he becomes a blackleg gambler and then it slams the door in his face.

God says, "Look out in the beginning for that thing." Society takes no note of the beginning. It waits until it becomes vice, and then it organizes Civic Righteousness clubs. Get back to the beginning and do your work there. God has planned to save this world through the preaching of men and women, and God reaches down to save men; he pulls them out of the grog shops and puts them on the water wagon.

I never could imagine an angel coming down from heaven and preaching to men and women to save them. God never planned to save this world with the preaching of angels. When Jesus Christ died on the cross he died to redeem those whose nature he took. An angel wouldn't know what he was up against. Some one would say: "Good Angel, were you ever drunk?" "No!" "Good Angel, did you ever swear?" "Oh, no!" "Good Angel, did you ever try to put up a stove-pipe in the fall?" "Oh, no!" "Did you ever stub your toe while walking the floor with the baby at three A.M.?" "Oh, no!"

Well, then, Mr. Angel, you don't know. You say there is great mercy with God, but you are not tempted."

No. God planned to save the world by saving men and women and letting them tell the story.

The servant of Naaman entered the hut of the prophet Elisha and found him sitting on a high stool writing with a quill pen on papyrus. The servant bowed low and said, "The great and mighty Naaman, captain of the hosts of the king of Syria, awaits thee. Unfortunately he is a leper and cannot enter your august presence. He has heard of the miraculous cures that you have wrought and he hopes to become the recipient of your power." The old prophet of God replied:

"Tell him to dip seven times in the Jordan—beat it, beat it, beat it." The servant came out to Naaman, who was sitting on his horse.

"Well, is he at home?"

"He's at home, but he is a queer duck."

Naaman thought that Elisha would come out and pat the sores and say incantations, like an Indian medicine man. Naaman was wroth, like many a fool today. God reveals to the sinner the plan of salvation and, instead of thanking God for salvation and doing what God wants him to do, he condemns God and everybody else for bothering him.

Now here is a man who wants to be a Christian. What will he do? Will he go ask some old saloon-keeper? Will he go ask some of these old brewers? Will he ask some of the fellows of the town? Will he ask the County Liquor Dealers' Association? Where will he go? To the preacher, of course. He is the man to go to when you want to be a Christian. Go to a doctor when you are sick, to a blacksmith when your horse is to be shod, but go to the preacher when you want your heart set right.

So Naaman goes into the muddy water and the water begins to lubricate those old sores, and it begins to itch, and he says, "Gee whizz," like many a young fellow today who goes to a church and just gets religion enough to make him feel miserable. An old fellow in Iowa came to me and said, "Bill, I have been to hear you every night and you have done me a lot of good. I used to cuss my old woman every day and I ain't cussed her for a week. I'm getting a little better."

The trouble with many men is that they have got just enough religion to make them miserable. If there is no joy in religion, you have got a leak in your religion. Some haven't religion enough to pay their debts. Would that I might have a hook and for every debt that you left unpaid I might jerk off a piece of clothing. If I did some of you fellows would have not anything on but a celluloid collar and a pair of socks.

Some of you have not got religion enough to have family prayer. Some of you people haven't got religion enough to take the beer bottles out of your cellar and throw them in the alley. You haven't got religion enough to tell that proprietor of the red light, "No, you can't rent my house after the first of June;" to tell the saloon-keeper, "You can't rent my house when your lease runs out"; and I want to tell you that the man that rents his property to a saloon-keeper is as low-down as the saloon-keeper. The trouble with you is that you are so taken up with business, with politics, with making money, with your lodges, and each and every one is so dependent on the other, that you are scared to death to come out and live clean cut for God Almighty. You have not fully surrendered yourself to God.

The matter with a lot of you people is that your religion is not complete. You have not yielded yourself to God and gone out for God and God's truth. Why, I am almost afraid to make some folks laugh for fear that I will be arrested for breaking a costly piece of antique bric-a-brac. You would think that if some people laughed it would break their faces. To see some people you would think that the essential of orthodox Christianity is to have a face so long you could eat oatmeal out of the end of a gas pipe. Sister, that is not religion; I want to tell you that the happy, smiling, sunny-faced religion will win more people to Jesus Christ than the miserable old grim-faced kind will in ten years. I pity anyone who can't laugh. There must be something wrong with their religion or their liver. The devil can't laugh.

So I can see Naaman as he goes into the water and dips seven times, and lo! his flesh becomes again as a little child's. When? When he did what God told him to do.

I have seen men come down the aisle by the thousands, men who have drank whisky enough to sink a ship. I have seen fallen women come to the front by scores and hundreds, and I have seen them go away cleansed by the power of God. When? When they did just what God told them to do.

I wish to God the Church were as afraid of imperfection as it is of perfection.

I saw a woman that for twenty-seven years had been proprietor of a disorderly house, and I saw her come down the aisle, close her doors, turn the girls out of her house and live for God. I saw enough converted in one town where there were four disorderly houses to close their doors; they were empty; the girls had all fled home to their mothers.

Out in Iowa a fellow came to me and spread a napkin on the platform —a napkin as big as a tablecloth. He said: "I want a lot of shavings and sawdust."

"What for?"

"I'll tell you; I want enough to make a sofa pillow. Right here is where I knelt down and was converted and my wife and four children, and my neighbors. I would like to have enough to make a sofa pillow to have something in my home to help me think of God. I don't want to forget God, or that I was saved. Can you give me enough?"

I said, "Yes, indeed, and if you want enough to make a mattress, all right, take it; and if you want enough of the tent to make a pair of breeches for each of the boys, why take your scissors and cut it right out, if it will help you to keep your mind on God."

That is why I like to have people come down to the front and publicly acknowledge God. I like to have a man have a definite experience in religion—something to remember.

A Plain Talk to Women

say to you, young girl, don't go with that godless, God-for-saken, sneering young man that walks the streets smoking cigarettes. He would not walk the streets with you if you smoked cigarettes. But you say you will marry him and re-form him; he would not marry you to reform you. Don't go to that dance. Don't you know that it is the most damnable, low-down institution on the face of God's earth, that it causes more ruin than anything this side of hell? Don't you go with that young man; don't you go to that dance. That is why we have so many whip-poor-will widows around the country: they married some of these mutts to reform them, and instead of doing that the undertaker got them. I say, young girl, don't go to that dance; it has proven to be the moral graveyard that has caused more ruination than anything that was ever spewed out of the mouth of hell. Don't go with that young fellow for a joy ride at midnight.

Girls, when some young fellow comes up and asks you the greatest question that you will ever be asked or called upon to answer, next to the salvation of your own soul, what will you say? "Oh, this is so sud-den!" That is all a bluff; you have been waiting for it all the time.

But, girls, never mind now, get down to facts. When he asks you the greatest question, the most important one that any girl is ever asked, next to the salvation of her soul, just say, "Sit down and let me ask you three questions. I want to ask you these three questions and if I am satisfied with your answer, it will determine my answer to your ques-tion. 'Did you believe me to be virtuous when you came here to ask me to be your wife?" "Oh, yes, I believed you to be virtuous. That's the reason I came here. You are like violets dipped in dew." The second question: "Have you as a young man lived as you demand of me as a girl that I should have lived?" The third question: "If I, as a girl, had lived and done as you, as a young man, and you knew it, would you ask me to marry you?"

They will line up and nine times out of ten they will take the count. You can line them up, and I know what I am talking about, and I defy any man on God's earth successfully to contradict me. I have the goods. The average young man is more particular about the company he keeps than the average girl. I'll tell you. If he meets somebody on the street whom he doesn't want to meet he will duck into the first open doorway and avoid the publicity of meeting her, for fear she might smile or give an indication that she had seen him somewhere and sometime before that. Yet our so-called best girls keep company with young men whose character would make a black mark on a piece of anthracite. Their characters are foul and rotten and damnable.

I like to see a girl who has a good head, and can choose right because it is right, never minding the criticism. Choose the good and be careful of good company and good conduct, and keep company with a good young fellow. Don't go with the fellow whose reputation is bad. Everybody knows it is bad, and if you are seen with him you will lose your reputation as well, although your virtue is intact; and they might as well take you to the graveyard and bury you, when your reputation is gone. When a man like that asks you to go with him, say to him that if he will live the way you want him to you will go with him. If he would take a stand like that there wouldn't be so many wrecks. If our women and girls would take higher stands and say, "No, no, we will not keep company with you unless you live the way I want you to," there would be better men. A lot of you women hold yourselves too cheaply. You are scared to death for fear you will be what the world irreverently calls "an old maid."

You remember the prophet Elisha and his journey to the school of prophets up to Mount Carmel. There was a woman who noticed the actions and conduct of the man of God and she said to her husband, "Let us build a little room and place therein a bed, and bowl and pitcher, that he may make it his home."

The suggestion evidently met with the approval of the husband, because ever afterward the man of God enjoyed this hospitality. I sometimes thought she might have been a new woman of the olden times, because no mention is made of the husband. You never hear of some old lobsters unless they are fortunate enough to marry a woman who does things and their name is always mentioned in connection with what the wife does.

You know there are homes in which the advent of one, two and possibly three children is considered a curse instead of a blessing. God, in his providence, has often denied the honor of maternity to some women. But there are married women who shrink from maternity, not because of ill health, but simply because they love ease, because they love fine garments and ability to flirt like a butterfly at some social function.

Crimes have been and are being committed; hands are stained with blood; and that very crime has made France the charnel house of the world. And America, we of our boasted intelligence and wealth, we are fast approaching the same doom, until or unless it behooves somebody with grit and courage to preach against the prevailing sins and run the risk of incurring the displeasure of people who divert public attention from their own vileness rather than condemn themselves for the way they are living. They say the man who is preaching against it is vulgar, rather than the man who did it.

I am sure there is not an angel in heaven that would not be glad to come to earth and be honored with motherhood if God would grant her that privilege. What a grand thing it must be, at the end of your earthly career, to look back upon a noble and godly life, knowing you did all you could to help leave this old world to God and made your contributions in tears and in prayers and taught your offspring to be God-fearing, so that when you went you would continue to produce your noble character in your children.

Society has just about put maternity out of fashion. When you stop to consider the average society woman I do not think maternity has lost anything. The humbler children are raised by their mothers instead of being turned over to a governess.

There are too many girls who marry for other causes than love. I think ambition, indulgence and laziness lead more girls to the altar than love—girls not actuated by love, but simply willing to pay the price of wifehood to wear fine clothes. They are not moved by the noble desires of manhood or womanhood.

Some girls marry for novelty and some girls marry for a home. Some fool mothers encourage girls to marry for ease so they can go to the matinee and buzz around. Some fool girls marry for money and some girls marry for society, because by connecting their name with a certain family's they go up a rung in the social ladder, and some girls marry young bucks to reform them—and they are the biggest fools in the bunch, because the bucks would not marry the girls to reform them.

You mothers are worse fools to encourage your daughter to marry some old lobster because his father has money and when he dies, maybe your daughter can have good clothes and ride in an auto instead of hoofing it. Look at the girls on the auction block today. Look at the awful battle the average stenographer and average clerk has to fight. You cannot work for six dollars a week and wear fine duds and be on the square as much as you are without having the people suspicious.

In a letter to Miss Borson, President Roosevelt said: "The man or woman who avoids marriage and has a heart so cold as to know no passion and a brain so shallow as to dislike having children is, in fact, a criminal."

Is it well with thee? Is it well with your husband? "The best man in the world," you answer. Very well; is it well with the child? I think its responsibilities are equal, if they don't outweigh its privileges, and when God is in the heart of the child, I don't wonder that that home is a haven of peace and rest.

I have no motive in preaching except the interest I have in the moral welfare of the people. There is not money enough to hire me to preach. I tell you, ladies, we have to do something more than wipe our eyes, and blow our nose, and say "Come to Jesus." Go out and shell the woods and make them let you know why they don't "come to Jesus."

I believe the time will come when sex hygiene will form part of the high-school curriculum. I would rather have my children taught sex hygiene than Greek and Latin. A lot of the high-school curriculum is mere fad. I think the time will come when our girls will be taught in classes with some graduated woman physician for an instructor.

Women live on a higher plane, morally, than men. No woman was ever ruined that some brute of a man did not take the initiative. Women have kept themselves purer than men. I believe a good woman is the best thing this side of heaven and a bad woman the worst thing this side of hell. I think woman rises higher and sinks lower than man. I think she is the most degraded on earth or the purest on earth.

Our homes are on the level with women. Towns are on the level with homes. What women are our homes will be; and what the town is, the men will be, so you hold the destiny of the nation.

I believe there is something unfinished in the make-up of a girl who does not have religion. The average girl today no longer looks forward to motherhood as the crowning glory of womanhood. She is turning her home into a gambling shop and a social beer-and-champagne-drinking joint, and her society is made up of poker players, champagne, wine and beer drinkers, grass-widowers and jilted jades and slander-mongers —that comprises the society of many a girl today. She is becoming a matinee-gadder and fudge-eater.

I wish I could make a girl that flirts see herself as others see her. If you make eyes at a man on the street he will pay you back. It doesn't mean that you are pretty. It means that if you don't care any more for yourself than that why should he? The average man will take a girl at her personal estimate of herself.

It takes a whole lot of nerve for a fellow to look a girl in the face and say, "Will you be my wife and partner, and help me fight the battle during life?" but I think it means a whole lot more to the girl who has to answer and fight that question. But the fool girl loafs around and waits to be chosen and takes the first chance she gets and seems to think that if they get made one, the laws of man can make them two again.

The divorce laws are damnable. America is first in many things that I love, but there are many things that are a disgrace. We lead the world in crime; and lead the world in divorce—we who boast of our culture.

Many a girl has found out after she is married that it would have been a good deal easier to die an old maid than to have said "yes," and become the wife of some cigarette-smoking, cursing, damnable libertine. They will launch the matrimonial boat and put the oars in and try it once for luck, anyway, and so we have many women praying for unconverted husbands.

I preached like this in a town once and the next day I heard of about five engagements that were broken. I can give you advice now, but if the knot is tied, the thing is done.

I am a Roman Catholic on divorce. There are a whole lot of things worse than living and dying an old maid and one of them is marrying the wrong man. So don't be one to do that.

Now, girls, don't simper and look silly when you speak about love. There is nothing silly about it, although some folks are silly because they are in love. Love is the noblest and purest gift of God to man and womankind. Don't let your actions advertise "Man Wanted, Quick." That is about the surest way not to get a man. You might get a thing with breeches on, but he is no man.

Many a woman is an old maid because she wanted to do her share of the courting. Don't get excited and want to hurry things along. If a man begins to act as though he is after you, the surest way to get him is just to make him feel you don't want him, unless you drive him off by appearing too indifferent.

And, girls, don't worry if you think you are not going to get a chance to marry. Some of the noblest men in the world have been bachelors and some of the noblest women old maids. And, woman, for God's sake, when you do get married, don't transfer the love God gave you to bestow on a little child to a Spitz dog or a brindle pup.

All great women are satisfied with their common sphere in life and think it is enough to fill the lot God gave them in this world as wife and mother. I tell you the devil and women can damn this world, and Jesus and women can save this old world. It remains with womanhood today to lift our social life to a higher plane.

Mothers, be more careful of your boys and girls. Explain these evils that contaminate our social life today. I have had women say to me, "Mr. Sunday, don't you think there is danger of talking too much to them when they are so young?" Not much; just as soon as a girl is able to know the pure from the impure she should be taught. Oh, mothers, mothers, you don't know what your girl is being led to by this false and mock modesty.

Don't teach your girls that the only thing in the world is to marry. Why, some girls marry infidels because they were not taught to say "I would not do it." A girl is a big fool to marry an infidel. God says, "Be ye not unequally yoked with unbelievers."

I believe there is a race yet to appear which will be as far superior in morals to us as we are superior to the morals in the days of Julius Caesar; but that race will never appear until God-fearing young men marry God-fearing girls and the offspring are God-fearing.

Culture will never save the world. If these miserable human vampires who feed and fatten upon the virtue of womanhood can get off with impunity; nay, more, be feasted and petted and coddled by society, we might as well back-pedal out and sink in shame, for we can never see to the heights nor command the respect of the great and good.

What paved the way for the downfall of the mightiest dynasties—proud and haughty Greece and imperial Rome? The downfall of their womanhood. The virtue of womanhood is the rampart wall of American civilization. Break that down and with the stones thereof you can pave your way to the hottest hell, and reeking vice and corruption.

Mother

The story of Moses is one of the most beautiful and fascinating in all the world. It takes a hold on us and never for an instant does it lose its interest, for it is so graphically told that once heard it is never forgotten.

I have often imagined the anxiety with which that child was born, for he came into the world with the sentence of death hanging over him, for Pharaoh had decreed that the male children should die. The mother defied even the command of the king and determined that the child should live, and right from the beginning the battle of right against might was fought at the cradle.

Moses' mother was a slave. She had to work in the brickyards or labor in the field, but God was on her side and she won, as the mother always wins with God on her side. Before going to work she had to choose some hiding place for her child, and she put his little sister, Miriam, on guard while she kept herself from being seen by the soldiers of Pharaoh, who were seeking everywhere to murder the Jewish male children. For three months she kept him hidden, possibly finding a new hiding place every few days. It is hard to imagine anything more difficult than to hide a healthy, growing baby, and he was hidden for three months. Now he was grown larger and more full of life and a more secure hiding place had to be found, and I can imagine this mother giving up her rest and sleep to prepare an ark for the saving of her child.

I believe the plan must have been formulated in heaven. I have often thought God must have been as much interested in that work as was the mother of Moses, for you can't make me believe that an event so important as that, and so far-reaching in its results, ever happened by luck or chance. Possibly God whispered the plan to the mother when she went to him in prayer and in her grief because she was afraid the sword of Pharaoh would murder her child. And how carefully the material out of which the ark was made had to be selected! I think every twig was carefully scrutinized in order that nothing poor might get into its composition, and the weaving of that ark, the mother's heart, her soul, her prayers, her tears, were interwoven.

Oh, if you mothers would exercise as much care over the company your children keep, over the books they read and the places they go, there would not be so many girls feeding the red-light district, nor so many boys growing up to lead criminal lives. And with what thanksgiving she must have poured out her heart when at last the work was done and the ark was ready to carry its precious cargo, more precious than if it was to hold the crown jewels of Egypt. And I can imagine the last night that baby was in the home. Probably some of you can remember when the last night came when baby was alive; you can remember the last night the coffin stayed, and the next day the pall-bearers and the hearse came. The others may have slept soundly, but there was no sleep for you, and I can imagine there was no sleep for Moses' mother.

> "There are whips and tops and pieces of string
>   And shoes that no little feet ever wear;
> There are bits of ribbon and broken wings
>   And tresses of golden hair.

> "There are dainty jackets that never are worn
>   There are toys and models of ships;
> There are books and pictures all faded and torn
>   And marked by fingers tips
> Of dimpled hands that have fallen to dust—
> Yet we strive to think that the Lord is just.

> "Yet a feeling of bitterness fills our soul;
>   Sometimes we try to pray,
> That the Reaper has spared so many flowers
>   And taken ours away.
> And we sometimes doubt if the Lord can know
> How our riven hearts did love them so

"But we think of our dear ones dead,
  Our children who never grow old,
And how they are waiting and watching for us
  In the city with streets of gold;
And how they are safe through all the years
  From sickness and want and war.
We thank the great God, with falling tears,
  For the things in the cabinet drawer."

Others in the house might have slept, but not a moment could she spare of the precious time allotted her with her little one, and all through the night she must have prayed that God would shield and protect her baby and bless the work she had done and the step she was about to take.

Some people often say to me: "I wonder what the angels do; how they employ their time?" I think I know what some of them did that night. You can bet they were not out to some bridge-whist party. They guarded that house so carefully that not a soldier of old Pharaoh ever crossed the threshold. They saw to it that not one of them harmed that baby.

At dawn the mother must have kissed him good-bye, placed him in the ark and hid him among the reeds and rushes, and with an aching heart and tear-dimmed eyes turned back again to the field and back to the brickyards to labor and wait to see what God would do. She had done her prayerful best, and when you have done that you can bank on God to give the needed help. If we only believed that with God all things are possible no matter how improbable, what unexpected answers the Lord would give to our prayers! She knew God would help her some way, but I don't think she ever dreamed that God would help her by sending Pharaoh's daughter to care for the child. It was no harder for God to send the princess than it was to get the mother to prepare the ark. What was impossible from her standpoint was easy for God.

Pharaoh's daughter came down to the water to bathe, and the ark was discovered, just as God wanted it to be, and one of her maids was sent to fetch it. You often wonder what the angels are doing. I think some of the angels herded the crocodiles on the other side of the Nile to keep them from finding Moses and eating him up. You can bank on it, all heaven was interested to see that not one hair of that baby's head was injured. There weren't devils enough in hell to pull one hair out of its head. The ark was brought and with feminine curiosity the daughter of Pharaoh had to look into it to see what was there, and when they removed the cover, there was lying a strong, healthy baby boy, kicking up his heels and sucking his thumbs, as probably most of us did when we were boys, and probably as you did when you were a girl. The baby looks up and weeps, and those tears blotted out all that was against it and gave it a chance for its life. I don't know, but I think an angel stood there and pinched it to make it cry, for it cried at the right time. Just as God plans. God always does things at the right time. Give God a chance; he may be a little slow at times, but he will always get around in time.

The tears of that baby were the jewels with which Israel was ransomed from Egyptian bondage. The princess had a woman's heart and when a woman's heart and a baby's tears meet, something happens that gives the devil cold feet. Perhaps the princess had a baby that had died, and the sight of Moses may have torn the wound open and made it bleed afresh. But she had a woman's heart, and that made her forget she was the daughter of Pharaoh and she was determined to give protection to that baby. Faithful Miriam (the Lord be praised for Miriam) saw the heart of the princess reflected in her face. Miriam had studied faces so much that she could read the princess' heart as plainly as if written in an open book, and she said to her: "Shall I go and get one of the Hebrew women to nurse the child for you?" and the princess said, "Go."

I see her little feet and legs fly as she runs down the hot, dusty road, and her mother must have seen her coming a mile away, and she ran to meet her own baby put back in her arms. And she was being paid Egyptian gold to take care of her own baby. See how the Lord does things? "Now you take this child and nurse it for me and I will pay you your wages." It was a joke on Pharaoh's daughter, paying Moses' mother for doing what she wanted to do more than anything else—nurse her own baby.

How quickly the mother was paid for these long hours of anxiety and alarm and grief, and if the angels know what is going on what a hilarious time there must have been in heaven when they saw Moses and Miriam back at home, under the protection of the daughter of Pharaoh. I imagine she dropped on her knees and poured out her heart to God, who had helped her so gloriously. She must have said: "Well, Lord, I knew you would help me. I knew you would take care of my baby when I made the ark and put him in it and put it in the water, but I never dreamed that you would put him back into my arms to take care of, so I would not have to work and slave in the field and make brick and be tortured almost to death for fear that the soldiers of Pharaoh would find my baby and kill him. I never thought you would soften the stony heart of Pharaoh and make him pay me for what I would rather do than anything else in this world." I expect to meet Moses' mother in heaven, and I am going to ask her how much old Pharaoh had to pay her for that job. I think that's one of the best jokes, that old sinner having to pay the mother to take care of her own baby. But I tell you, if you give God a chance, he will fill your heart to overflowing. Just give him a chance.

This mother had remarkable pluck. Everything was against her but she would not give up. Her heart never failed. She made as brave a fight as any man ever made at the sound of the cannon or the roar of musketry.

> "The bravest battle that was ever fought,
>   Shall I tell you where and when?
> On the maps of the world you'll find it not—
>   'Twas fought by the mothers of men.
>
> "Nay, not with cannon or battle shot,
>   With sword or noble pen,
> Nay, not with the eloquent word or thought,
>   From the mouths of wonderful men.
>
> "But deep in the walled-up woman's heart—
>   Of women that would not yield.
> But, bravely, silently bore their part—
>   Lo, there is the battle-field.
>
> "No marshaling troops, no bivouac song,
>   No banner to gleam and wave;
> But oh, these battles they last so long—
>   From babyhood to the grave."

Mothers are always brave when the safety of their children is concerned.

This incident happened out West. A mother was working in a garden and the little one was sitting under a tree in the yard playing. The mother heard the child scream; she ran, and a huge snake was wrapping its coils about the baby, and as its head swung around she leaped and grabbed it by the neck and tore it from her baby and hurled it against a tree.

Fathers often give up. The old man often goes to boozing, becomes dissipated, takes a dose of poison and commits suicide; but the mother will stand by the home and keep the little band together if she has to manicure her finger nails over a washboard to do it. If men had half as much grit as the women there would be different stories written about a good many homes. Look at her work! It is the greatest in the world; in its far-reaching importance it is transcendentally above everything in the universe—her task in molding hearts and lives and shaping character. If you want to find greatness don't go to the throne, go to the cradle; and the nearer you get to the cradle the nearer you get to greatness. Now, when Jesus wanted to give his disciples an impressive object lesson he called in a college professor, did he? Not much. He brought in a little child and said: "Except ye become as one of these, ye shall in no wise enter the kingdom of God." The work is so important that God will not trust anybody with it but a mother. The launching of a boy or a girl to live for Christ is greater work than the launching of a battleship.

Moses was a chosen vessel of the Lord and God wanted him to get the right kind of a start, so he gave him a good mother. There wasn't a college professor in all Egypt that God would trust with that baby! so he put the child back in its mother's arms. He knew the best one on earth to trust with that baby was its own mother. When God sends us great men he wants to have them get the right kind of a start. So he sees to it that they have a good mother. Most any old stick will do for a daddy. God is particular about the mothers.

And so the great need of this country, or any other country, is good mothers, and I believe we have more good mothers in America than any other nation on earth. If Washington's mother had been like a Happy Hooligan's mother, Washington would have been a Happy Hooligan.

Somebody has said: "God could not be everywhere, so he gave us mothers." Now there may be poetry in it, but it's true "that the hand that rocks the cradle rules the world," and if every cradle was rocked by a good mother, the world would be full of good men, as sure as you breathe. If every boy and every girl today had a good mother, the saloons and disreputable houses would go out of business tomorrow.

A young man one time joined a church and the preacher asked him: "What was it I said that induced you to be a Christian?"

Said the young man: "Nothing that I ever heard you say, but it is the way my mother lived." I tell you an ounce of example outweighs forty million tons of theory and speculation. If the mothers would live as they should, we preachers would have little to do. Keep the devil out of the boys and girls and he will get out of the world. The old sinners will die off if we keep the young ones clean.

The biggest place in the world is that which is being filled by the people who are closely in touch with youth. Being a king, an emperor or a president is mighty small potatoes compared to being a mother or the teacher of children, whether in a public school or in a Sunday school, and they fill places so great that there isn't an angel in heaven that wouldn't be glad to give a bushel of diamonds to boot to come down here and take their places. Commanding an army is little more than sweeping a street or pounding an anvil compared with the training of a boy or girl. The mother of Moses did more for the world than all the kings that Egypt ever had. To teach a child to love truth and hate a lie, to love purity and hate vice, is greater than inventing a flying machine that will take you to the moon before breakfast. Unconsciously you set in motion influences that will damn or bless the old universe and bring new worlds out of chaos and transform them for God.

A man sent a friend of mine some crystals and said: "One of these crystals as large as a pin point will give a distinguishable green hue to sixteen hogsheads of water." Think of it! Power enough in an atom to tincture sixteen hogsheads of water. There is power in a word or act to blight a boy and, through him, curse a community. There is power enough in a word to tincture the life of that child so that it will become a power to lift the world to Jesus Christ. The mothers will put in motion influences that will either touch heaven or hell. Talk about greatness!

Oh, you wait until you reach the mountains of eternity, then read the mothers' names in God's hall of fame, and see what they have been in this world. Wait until you see God's hall of fame; you will see women bent over the washtub.

I want to tell you women that fooling away your time hugging and kissing a poodle dog, caressing a "Spitz," drinking society brandy-mash and a cocktail, and playing cards, is mighty small business compared to molding the life of a child.

Tell me, where did Moses get his faith? From his mother. Where did Moses get his backbone to say: "I won't be called the son of Pharaoh's daughter?" He got it from his mother. Where did Moses get the nerve to say, "Excuse me, please," to the pleasures of Egypt? He got it from his mother. You can bank on it he didn't inhale it from his dad. Many a boy would have turned out better if his old dad had died before the kid was born. You tell your boy to keep out of bad company. Sometimes when he walks down the street with his father he's in the worst company in town. His dad smokes, drinks and chews. Moses got it from his mother. He was learned in all the wisdom of Egypt, but that didn't give him the swelled head.

When God wants to throw a world out into space, he is not concerned about it. The first mile that world takes settles its course for eternity. When God throws a child out into the world he is mighty anxious that it gets a good start. The Catholics are right when they say: "Give us the children until they are ten years old and we don't care who has them after that." The Catholics are not losing any sleep about losing men and women from their church membership. It is the only church that has ever shown us the only sensible way to reach the masses—that is, by getting hold of the children. That's the only way on God's earth that you will ever solve the problem of reaching the masses. You get the boys and girls started right, and the devil will hang a crape on his door, bank his fires, and hell will be for rent before the Fourth of July.

A friend of mine has a little girl that she was compelled to take to the hospital for an operation. They thought she would be frightened, but she said: "I don't care if mama will be there and hold my hand." They prepared her for the operation, led her into the room, put her on the table, put the cone over her face and saturated it with ether, and she said: "Now, mama, take me by the hand and hold it and I'll not be afraid."

And the mother stood there and held her hand. The operation was performed, and when she regained consciousness, they said: "Bessie, weren't you afraid when they put you on the table?" She said: "No, mama stood there and held my hand. I wasn't afraid."

There is a mighty power in a mother's hand. There's more power in a woman's hand than there is in a king's scepter.

And there is a mighty power in a mother's kiss—inspiration, courage, hope, ambition, in a mother's kiss. One kiss made Benjamin West a painter, and the memory of it clung to him through life. One kiss will drive away the fear in the dark and make the little one brave. It will give strength where there is weakness.

I was in a town one day and saw a mother out with her boy, and he had great steel braces on both legs, to his hips, and when I got near enough to them I learned by their conversation that that wasn't the first time the mother had had him out for a walk. She had him out exercising him so he would get the use of his limbs. He was struggling and she smiled and said: "You are doing finely today; better than you did yesterday." And she stooped and kissed him, and the kiss of encouragement made him work all the harder, and she said: "You are doing nobly, son." And he said: "Mama, I'm going to run; look at me." And he started, and one of his toes caught on the steel brace on the other leg and he stumbled, but she caught him and kissed him, and said: "That was fine, son; how well you did it!" Now, he did it because his mother had encouraged him with a kiss. He didn't do it to show off. There is nothing that will help and inspire life like a mother's kiss.

"If we knew the baby fingers pressed against the window pane,
  Would be cold and still tomorrow, never trouble us again,
  Would the bright eyes of our darling catch the frown upon our brow?

"Let us gather up the sunbeams lying all around our path,
  Let us keep the wheat and roses, casting out the thorns and chaff!
  We shall find our sweetest comforts in the blessings of today,
  With a patient hand removing all the briars from our way."

There is power in a mother's song, too. It's the best music the world has ever heard. The best music in the world is like biscuits—it's the kind mother makes. There is no brass band or pipe organ that can hold a candle to mother's song. Calve, Melba, Nordica, Eames, Schumann-Heinck, they are cheap skates, compared to mother. They can't sing at all. They don't know the rudiments of the kind of music mother sings. The kind she sings gets tangled up in your heart strings. There would be a disappointment in the music of heaven to me if there were no mothers there to sing. The song of an angel or a seraph would not have much charm for me. What would you care for an angel's song if there were no mother's song?

The song of a mother is sweeter than that ever sung by minstrel or written by poet. Talk about sonnets! You ought to hear the mother sing when her babe is on her breast, when her heart is filled with emotion. Her voice may not please an artist, but it will please any one who has a heart in him. The songs that have moved the world are not the songs written by the great masters. The best music, in my judgment, is not the faultless rendition of these high-priced opera singers. There is nothing in art that can put into melody the happiness which associations and memories bring. I think when we reach heaven it will be found that some of the best songs we will sing there will be those we learned at mother's knee.

There is power in a mother's love. A mother's love must be like God's love. How God could ever tell the world that he loved it without a mother's help has often puzzled me. If the devils in hell ever turned pale, it was the day mother's love flamed up for the first time in a woman's heart. If the devil ever got "cold feet" it was that day, in my judgment.

You know a mother has to love her babe before it is born. Like God, she has to go into the shadows of the valley of death to bring it into the world, and she will love her child, suffer for it, and it can grow up and become vile and yet she will love it. Nothing will make her blame it, and I think, women, that one of the awful things in hell will be that there will be no mother's love there. Nothing but black, bottomless, endless, eternal hate in hell—no mother's love.

> "And though he creep through the vilest caves of sin,
>   And crouch perhaps, with bleared and blood-shot eyes,
>   Under the hangman's rope—a mother's lips
>   Will kiss him in his last bed of disgrace,
>   And love him e'en for what she hoped of him."

I thank God for what mother's love has done for the world.

Oh, there is power in a mother's trust. Surely as Moses was put in his mother's arms by the princess, so God put the babes in your arms, as a charge from him to raise and care for. Every child is put in a mother's arms as a trust from God, and she has to answer to God for the way she deals with that child. No mother on God's earth has any right to raise her children for pleasure. She has no right to send them to dancing school and haunts of sin. You have no right to do those things that will curse your children. That babe is put in our arms to train for the Lord. No mother has any more right to raise her children for pleasure than I have to pick your pockets or throw red pepper in your eyes. She has no more right to do that than a bank cashier has to rifle the vaults and take the savings of the people. One of the worst sins you can commit is to be unfaithful to your trust.

"Take this child and nurse it for me." That is all the business you have with it. That is a jewel that belongs to God and he gives it to you to polish for him so he can set it in a crown. Who knows but that Judas became the godless, good-for-nothing wretch he was because he had a godless, good-for-nothing mother? Do you know? I don't. What is more to blame for the crowded prisons than mothers? Who is more to blame for the crowded disreputable houses than you are, who let your children gad the streets, with every Tom, Dick and Harry, or keep company with some little jack rabbit whose character would make a black mark on a piece of tar paper? I have talked with men in prisons who have damned their mothers to my face. Why? They blame their mothers for their being where they are.

"Take the child and nurse it for me, and I will pay you your wages." God pays in joy that is fire-proof, famine-proof and devil-proof. He will pay you, don't you worry. So get your name on God's pay-roll. "Take this child and nurse it for me, and I will pay you your wages." If you haven't been doing that, then get your name on God's pay-roll.

"Take this child and nurse it for me, and I will pay you your wages." Then your responsibility! It is so great that I don't see how any woman can fail to be a Christian and serve God. What do you think God will do if the mother fails? I stagger under it. What, if through your unfaithfulness, your boy becomes a curse and your daughter a blight? What, if through your neglect, that boy becomes a Judas when he might have been a John or Paul?

Down in Cincinnati some years ago a mother went to the zoological garden and stood leaning over the bear pit, watching the bears and dropping crumbs and peanuts to them. In her arms she held her babe, a year and three months old. She was so interested in the bears that the baby wriggled itself out of her arms and fell into the bear pit, and she watched those huge monsters rip it to shreds. What a veritable hell it will be through all her life to know that her little one was lost through her own carelessness and neglect!

"Take this child and raise it for me, and I will pay you your wages." Will you promise and covenant with God, and with me, and with one another, that from now on you will try, with God's help, to do better than you ever have done to raise your children for God?

I once read the story of an angel who stole out of heaven and came to this world one bright, sunshiny day; roamed through field, forest, city and hamlet, and as the sun went down plumed his wings for the return flight. The angel said: "Now that my visit is over, before I return I must gather some mementos of my trip." He looked at the beautiful flowers in the garden and said: "How lovely and fragrant," and plucked the rarest roses, made a bouquet, and said: "I see nothing more beautiful and fragrant than these flowers." The angel looked farther and saw a bright-eyed, rosy-cheeked child, and said: "That baby is prettier than the flowers; I will take that, too," and looking behind to the cradle, he saw a mother's love pouring out over her babe like a gushing spring, and the angel said: "The mother's love is the most beautiful thing I have seen! I will take that, too."

And with these three treasures the heavenly messenger winged his flight to the pearly gates, saying: "Before I go I must examine the mementos of my trip to the earth." He looked at the flowers; they had withered. He looked at the baby's smile, and it had faded. He looked at the mother's love, and it shone in all its pristine beauty. Then he threw away the withered flowers, cast aside the faded smile, and with the mother's love pressed to his breast, swept through the gates into the city, shouting that the only thing he had found that would retain its fragrance from earth to heaven was a mother's love.

"Take this child and nurse it for me, and I will pay you your wages."

When Napoleon Bonaparte was asked, "What do you regard as the greatest need of France?" he replied, "Mothers, mothers, mothers." You women can make a hell of a home or a heaven of a home. Don't turn your old Gatling-gun tongue loose and rip everybody up and rip your husbands up and send them out of their homes. If I were going to investigate your piety I would ask the girl who works for you.

This talk about the land of the free is discounted when the children look like a rummage sale in a secondhand store; with uncombed hair, ripped pants, buttons off, stockings hanging down. It doesn't take the wisdom of truth to see that mother is too busy with her social duties, clubs, etc., to pay much attention to the kids.

The mother of Nero was a murderess, and it is no wonder that he fiddled while Rome burned. The mother of Patrick Henry was eloquent, and that is the reason why every school boy and girl knows, "Give me liberty or give me death." Coleridge's mother taught him Biblical stories from the old Dutch tile of the fireplace. In the home authority is needed today more than at any time in the history of this nation. I have met upon the arena of the conflict every form of man and beast imaginable to meet, and I am convinced that neither law nor gospel can make a nation without home authority and home example. Those two things are needed. The boy who has a wholesome home and surroundings and a judicious control included does not often find his way into the reformatory.

Susanna Wesley was the mother of nineteen children, and she held them for God. When asked how she did it she replied, "By getting hold of their hearts in their youth, and never losing my grip."

If it had not been for the expostulations of the mother of George Washington, George Washington would have become a midshipman in the British navy, and the name of that capital yonder would have been some other. John Randolph said in the House of Representatives, "If it had not been for my godly mother, I, John Randolph, would have been an infidel." Gray, who wrote the "Elegy in a Country Church-yard," said he was one of a large family of children that had the misfortune to survive their mother. And I believe the ideal mother is the product of a civilization that rose from the manger of Bethlehem.

I am sure there is not an angel in heaven that would not be glad to come to earth and be honored with motherhood if God would grant that privilege. What a grand thing it must be, at the end of your earthly career, to look back upon a noble and godly life, knowing you did all you could to help leave this old world to God, and made your contributions in tears and in prayers and taught your offspring to be God-fearing, so that when you went you would continue to produce your noble character in your children.

I believe in blood; I believe in good blood, bad blood, honest blood, and thieving blood; in heroic blood and cowardly blood; in virtuous blood, in licentious blood, in drinking blood and in sober blood. The lips of Hapsburgs tell of licentiousness; those of the Stuarts tell of cruelty, bigotry and sensuality, from Mary, queen of Scots, down to Charles the First and Charles the Second, James the First—who showed the world what your fool of a Scotchman can be when he is a fool— down to King James the Second.

Scotch blood stands for stubbornness. They are full of stick-to-it-iveness. I know, Mrs. Sunday is full-blooded Scotch. English blood speaks of reverence for the English. That is shown by the fact that England spent $50,000,000 recently to put a crown on George's head. Danish blood tells of love of the sea. Welsh blood tell of religious fervor and zeal for God. Jewish blood tells of love of money, from the days of Abraham down until now.

You may have read this story: Down in New York was a woman who said to her drunken son: "Let's go down to the police court and have the judge send you over to the island for a few weeks. Maybe you'll straighten up then and I can have some respect for you again." Down they went to the police court and appeared before the judge. He asked who would make the charge and the mother sprang forward with the words on her lips. Then she stopped short, turned to her son and throwing her arms about his neck cried out: "I can't! I can't! He is my son, I love him and I can't." Then she fell at his feet dead. As dearly as she had loved her drunken, bloated, loafing son she couldn't stand in judgment.

The Holy Spirit

The personality, the divinity and the attributes of the Holy Ghost afford one of the most inspiring, one of the most beneficial examples in our spiritual life. We are told that when the Holy Spirit came at Pentecost, he came as the rushing of a mighty wind and overurging expectancy. When Jesus was baptized in the River Jordan, of John, out from the expanse of heaven was seen to float the Spirit of God like a snow-flake, and they heard a sound as of whirring wings, and the Holy Spirit in the form of a dove hovered over the dripping locks of Christ. Neither your eyes nor mine will ever behold such a scene; neither will our ears ever hear such a sound again. You cannot dissect or weigh the Holy Spirit, nor analyze him as a chemist may analyze material matter in his laboratory, but we can all feel the pulsing of the breath of his eternal love.

The Holy Spirit is a personality; as much a personality as Christ, or you or I. "Howbeit, when he, the Spirit of truth, is come, he will guide you into all truth: for he shall not speak of himself." He is to us what Jesus was when he was on earth. Jesus always speaks of the Holy Spirit in the future tense. He said, "It is expedient that I go away; if I go not away the Spirit will not come. It is expedient for you that I go away, but when I am gone, then I will send Him unto you who is from the Father." So we are living today in the beneficence of the Holy Spirit.

I do not believe in this twentieth-century theory of the universal fatherhood of God and the brotherhood of man. We are all made of one blood—that is true, physically speaking; we are all related. I am talking about the spiritual, not the physical. You are not a child of God unless you are a Christian; then you are a child of God—if you are a Christian.

Samson with the Holy Spirit upon him could take the jawbone of an

160 and lay dead a thousand Philistines. Samson without the Holy Spirit was as weak as a newborn babe, and they poked his eyes out and cut off his locks. And so with the Church and her members. Without the Holy Spirit you are as sounding brass and tinkling cymbals, simply four walls and a roof, and a pipe organ and a preacher to do a little stunt on Sunday morning and evening. I tell you, Christian people, that with the Holy Spirit there is no power on earth or in hell that can stand before the Church of Jesus Christ. And the damnable, hell-born, whisky-soaked, hog-jowled, rum-soaked moral assassins have damned this community long enough. Now it is time it was broken up and it is time to do something.

There are three classes in the Church, as I have looked at it from my standpoint. The first are those in the Church personally who want to be saved, but they are not concerned about other people. They do not give any help to other people; they don't lie awake at night praying for other people that they may be brought to the Lord.

The second class are going to depend upon human wisdom. There is no such thing as latent power, expressed or implied—power is just as distinctive in an individual as the electricity in these lights. If these globes are without a current they would be nothing but glass bulbs, fit for nothing but the scrap heap. Without the Holy Spirit you are as sounding brass and tinkling cymbals, and a third-rate amusement parlor, with religion left out.

The third class are church members not from might and honor and power, but from the Spirit.

While at Pentecost one sermon saved 3,000 people, now it takes 3,000 sermons to get one old buttermilk-eyed, whisky-soaked blasphemer.

We have our churches, our joss houses, our tabernacles; we have got the wisdom of the orientals, the ginger, vim, tabasco sauce, peppering of the twentieth century; we have got all of that, and I do not believe that there are any people beneath the sun who are better fed, better paid, better clothed, better housed, or any happier than we are beneath the stars and stripes—no nation on earth. There are lots of things that could be eliminated to make us better than we are today. We are the happiest people in God's world.

Out in Iowa, a fellow said to me: "Mr. Sunday, we ought to be better organized." Just think of that, we ought to be better organized.

Now listen to me, my friends! Listen to me! There is so much machinery in the churches today that you can hear it squeak.

Drop into a young people's meeting. The leader will say in a weak, effeminate, apologetic, minor sort of way, that there was a splendid topic this evening but he had not had much time for preparation. It is superfluous for him to say that; you could have told that. He goes along and tells how happy he is to have you there to take part this evening, making this meeting interesting. Some one gets up and reads a poem from the *Christian Endeavor World* and then they sing No. 38. They get up and sing:

> "*Oh, to be nothing—nothing,*
> *Only to lie at His feet.*"

We used to sing that song, but I found out that people took it so literally that I cut it out.

> "*Throw out the life line,*
> *Throw out the life line.*"

They haven't got strength enough to put up a clothesline. Another long pause, and then you hear, "Have all taken part that feel free to do so? We have a few minutes left. So let us sing No. 23." Then another long pause. "I hear the organ prelude; it is time for us to close, now let us all repeat together, 'The Lord keep watch between me and thee, while we are absent one from another.'"

I tell you God has got a hard job on his hands. Ever hear anything like that?

Believe that God Almighty can do something. Don't whine around as though God were a corpse, ready for the undertaker. God is still on the job. The Holy Spirit is needed to bring man into spiritual touch with God; to make man realize that he is a joint representative of God on earth today. Do you ever realize that you are God's representative— God's ambassador?

And as we are God's ambassadors why should we fear what the devil may do? Can it be that you fail to realize his power? Or are you so blind to the spiritual that you can't see that you need God's help? Let me ask you one question: Are you ready to surrender to him? A man said to me: "It was a mighty little thing to drive Adam and Eve out of the Garden of Eden because they ate an apple." It wasn't the fruit. It was the principle, whether man should bow to God or God bow to man. That act was an act of disobedience. You may say it was a mighty little thing for England to go to war with us because we threw some tea into Boston harbor. We didn't go to war over the tea. We said: "You can't brew tea in the East India Company and pour it down our throats." It was the principle we went to war about, not the price of tea, and we fought it out. Are you ready to surrender? You, who are in rebellion against God? You, who are in rebellion against the authority of God's government? Are you ready to do his will?

A good many people suppose that when they have accepted Jesus Christ as their Saviour and joined the Church that is all there is to the Christian life. As well might a student who has just matriculated imagine that he has finished his education. Nobody has reached a stage in the Christian life from which he cannot go further unless he is in the coffin—and then it's all over. To accept Christ, to join the Church, is only to begin. It is the starting of the race, not the reaching of the goal. There are constant and increasing blessings if you are willing to pay the price.

I don't care when or where you became a church member, if the Comforter, who is the Holy Ghost, is not with you, you are a failure.

This power of the Spirit is meant for all who are Christians. It is a great blessing for the Presbyterian elder as well as for the preacher. I know some Methodist stewards who need it. Deacons would "deak" better if they had it. It is a great blessing for the deacon and the members of the prudential committee, and it is just as great a blessing for the man in the pew who holds no office. To hear some people talk you would think that the Holy Spirit is only for preachers. God sets no double standard for the Christian life. There's nothing in the Bible to show that the people may live differently from the man in the pulpit.

I once heard a doctor of divinity pray for the Holy Spirit, and he said: "Send it upon us now." He was wrong, doubly wrong. The Holy Spirit is not an impersonal thing. He is a person, not an "it." And the Holy Spirit has always been here since the days of Pentecost. He does not come and go. He is right here in the world and his power is at the command of all who will put themselves into position to use it.

A university professor was greeted by a friend of mine who took him by the hand, and said: "What do you think of the Holy Spirit?" The professor answered that he regarded the Holy Spirit as an influence for good, a sort of emanation from God. My friend talked to him and tried to show him his mistake, and a few months later he met him again. "What do you think of the Holy Spirit now?" he asked. The professor answered: "Well, I know that the Holy Spirit is a person. Since I talked with you and have come to that conviction, I have succeeded in bringing sixty-three students to Christ."

A great many people think the Holy Spirit comes and goes again, and quote from the Acts, where it says that Peter was filled with the Holy Spirit. Well, if you will find that Peter had been doing things right along, that showed he had been filled with the Holy Spirit all the time. Acts, second chapter and fourth verse, we read: "And they were all filled with the Holy Spirit." You have no right, nor have I, to say that the Holy Spirit ever left any one. We have no right to seek to find Scripture to bolster up some little theory of our own. We must take Word of God for it, just as we find it written there. Now, at Pentecost, Peter had said: "Repent, and be baptized for the remission of sins." Then he promised them that the Holy Spirit would come and fill them. Now we have the fulfilment of the promise.

Who were filled with the Holy Spirit? Peter and James and John? No—the people. That is the record of the filling with the Holy Spirit of the three thousand who were converted at Pentecost, not the filling of Peter and James and John.

If the Spirit remains forever, why doesn't his power always show itself? Why haven't you as much power with God as the one hundred and twenty had at Pentecost? There are too many frauds, too much trash in the Church. It is because the people are not true to God. They are disobeying him. They are not right with him yet.

I don't know just how the Holy Spirit will come, but Jesus said we should do even greater works than he did. What are you doing? You are not doing such works now.

We find the Holy Spirit in the Old Testament. When the prophets spoke they were moved by him. God seems to have spoken to man in three distinct dispensations. Once it was through the covenant with Abraham, then it was through Moses and under the Mosaic dispensation, and finally it is through his own son, Jesus Christ. Jesus Christ came into the world, proved that he is the Son of God, suffered, died and was buried, rose again, and sent his Holy Comforter. This is the last dispensation. There is no evidence that after the Holy Spirit once came, he ever left the world. He is here now, ready to help you to overcome your pride, and your diffidence that has kept you from doing personal work, and is willing and ready to lead you into a closer relationship with Jesus.

But you say, some are elected and some are not. On that point I agree with Henry Ward Beecher. He said: "The elect are those who will and the non-elect are those who won't."

But you go in for culture—"culchah." If you are too cultured to be a Christian, God pity you. You may call it culture. I have another name for it. Is there anything about Christianity that is necessarily uncultured? I think the best culture in the world is among the followers of Jesus Christ.

But you say: "Ignorance is a bar to some." No sir. Billy Bray, the Cornish miner, was an illiterate man. He was asked if he could read writing, and he answered: "No, I can't even read readin'." Yet Billy Bray did a wonderful work for God in Wales and England. Ignorance is no bar to religion, or to usefulness for Jesus.

Some time ago, over in England, a man died in the poor house. He had had a little property, just a few acres of land, and it hadn't been enough to support him. After he died the new owner dug a well on it, and at a depth of sixty-five feet he found a vein of copper so rich that it meant a little fortune. If the man who died had only known of that vein, he need not have lived in poverty. There are many who are just as ignorant of the great riches within their reach. Lots of people hold checks on the bank of heaven, and haven't faith enough to present them at the window to have them cashed.

You may say, "I have failed in something, but it is a little thing." Oh, these little things! Bugs are little things, but they cost this country $800,000,000 in one year. Birds are little enemies of the bugs, and birds are little things, and if it weren't for the birds we would starve in two years. If there's anything that makes me mad it is to see a farmer grab a shotgun and kill a chicken hawk. That hawk is worth a lot more than some old hen you couldn't cook tender if you boiled it for two days. That chicken hawk has killed all the gophers, mice and snakes it could get its claws on and it has come to demand from the farmer the toll that is rightfully due to it, for what it has done to rid the land of pests.

Why is it that with all our universities and colleges we haven't produced a book like the Bible? It was written long ago by people who lived in a little country no bigger than some of our states. The reason was that God was behind the writers. The book was inspired.

When good old Dr. Backus, of Hamilton College, lay dying the doctor whispered to Mrs. Backus, saying, "Dr. Backus is dying." The old man heard and looked up with a smile on his face and asked: "Did I understand you to say that I am dying?"

Sadly the doctor said: "Yes, I'm sorry, you have no more than half an hour to live."

Dr. Backus smiled again. "Then it will soon be over," he said. "Take me out of bed and put me on my knees. I want to die praying for the students of Hamilton College." They lifted him out and he knelt down and covered his face with his transparent hands, and prayed "Oh, God, save the students of Hamilton College."

For a time he continued to pray, then the doctor said, "He is getting weaker." They lifted him back upon the bed, and his face was whiter than the pillows. Still his lips moved. "Oh, God, save——" Then the light of life went out, and he finished the prayer in the presence of Jesus. What did his dying prayer do? Why, almost the entire student body of Hamilton College accepted Jesus Christ.

If you haven't the power of the Spirit you have done something wrong. I don't know what it is—it's none of my business. It's between you and God. It is only my duty to call upon you to confess and get right with him.

A man went to a friend of mine and said: "I don't know what is wrong with me. I teach a Sunday-school class of young men, and I have tried to bring them to Jesus, and I have failed. Can you tell me why?"

"Yes," was the answer. "There's something wrong with you. You've done something wrong."

The man hesitated, but finally he said, "You're right. Years ago I was cashier in a big business house, and one time the books balanced and there was some money left over. I took that money and I have kept it. That was twelve years ago. Here is the money in this envelope."

"Take it back to the owner," said my friend. "It's not yours, and it's not mine."

"But I can't do that," said the man. "I am making a salary of $22,000 a year now, and I have a wife and daughters, and my firm will never employ a dishonest man."

"Well, that's your business," said my friend. "I have advised you, and that's all I can do; but God will never forgive you until you've given that money back."

The man sank into a chair and covered his eyes for a while. Then he got up and said, "I'll do it." He took a Chesapeake and Ohio train and went to Philadelphia, and went to a great merchant prince in whose employ he had been, and told his story. The merchant prince shut and locked the door. "Let us pray," he said. They knelt together, the great merchant's arm about his visitor; and when they got up the great merchant said: "Go in peace, God bless you."

On the next Sunday the man who had confessed took the Bible on his knee as he sat before his class and said to them: "Young men, I often wondered why I couldn't win any of you to Christ. My life was wrong, and I've repented and made it right." That man won his entire class for Christ, and they joined Dr. McKibben's church at Walnut Hills, Cincinnati, Ohio.

If you would get right with God what would be the result? Why, you would save your city.

Some time ago the funeral of a famous woman was held in London. Edward, who was king then, came with his consort, Alexandra, to look upon her face, and dukes and duchesses and members of the nobility came. Then the doors were opened and the populace came in by thousands. Down the aisle came a woman whose face and dress bore the marks of poverty. By one hand she led a child, and in her arms she carried another. As she reached the coffin she set down the child she was carrying and bent her head upon the glass above the quiet face in the coffin, and her old fascinator fell down upon it.

"Come," said a policeman, "you must move on."

But the woman stood by the coffin. "I'll not move on," she said, "for I have a right here."

The policeman said, "You must move on. It's orders"; but the woman said, "No, I've walked sixty miles to look upon her face again. She saved my two boys from being drunkards." The woman in the coffin was Mrs. Booth, wife of the great leader of the Salvation Army.

I'd rather have some reclaimed drunkard, or some poor girl redeemed from sin and shame, stand by my coffin and rain down tears of gratitude upon it, than to have a monument of gold studded with precious stones, that would pierce the skies.

"If ye love me keep my commandments. And I will pray the Father, and he shall give you another Comforter, that he may abide with you forever."

The Three Groups

od created man and placed him in the Garden of Eden, and gave him an explicit command, and man disobeyed, with the full knowledge of the penalty ringing in his ears, for God said: "In the day thou eatest of the fruit thou shalt surely die."

The Lord did not mean a period of twenty-four hours, but did mean that man would pass a crisis in his career. Adam ate of the forbidden fruit, and this world became a graveyard. If man had not sinned we never would have died. All the misery, all the disease, all the heartaches have come through sin. The hearse backs up in front of our homes and drives away with our loved ones because of sin.

But when man sinned God gave the promise, "The seed of the woman shall bruise the serpent's head." In the fullness of time Jesus came into the world in fulfillment of that promise. He opened the eyes of the blind, stilled the tempest, fed the multitude with five loaves and two fishes, cast out devils and raised the dead. He demonstrated by word and deed that He was the Son of God. The Jews spurned and repudiated His claim, and their enmity finally culminated in His crucifixion. But before that heartrending tragedy was enacted several incidents occurred, from one of which I take my text.

Jesus said to His disciples, "Go your way into the village over against you, and you will find a colt tied whereon never man sat; loose him and bring him to Me. And if any man ask you, Why do ye this? say The Lord hath need of him; and straightway he will send him hither." And the disciples went their way and found the colt tied in front of a house where two ways met, and there was a crowd of men loafing about the place; and if they were in any way like the bunch in our day, they were whittling, cursing, chewing tobacco, discussing financial, political and all other public questions.

The disciples began untying the colt, when one fellow, who spits tobacco juice enough to drown a rabbit, calls out, "Hey there! What are you doing? What are you going to do with that colt?" The disciples call back: "The Lord hath need of him." So away they go with the colt to where Jesus was and He on its back enters the city of Jerusalem on His famous triumphal entry.

A great multitude followed, shouting, "Hosanna to the son of David! Blessed is He that cometh in the name of the Lord! They spread their garments on the ground in front of Jesus. They cut down branches from the trees; they paved His way with flowers. You would have thought by their acclaim that then and there they would crown Him, but let us wait and see.

Jesus said to Peter and John, "You go on, and you will meet a man bearing a pitcher of water. You follow him into the house he enters, and say to the goodman of the house, "Where is the guest chamber?' He will show you an upper room furnished; there make ready."

Jesus desired to eat the Passover feast with His disciples, commemorating the passing over of the destroying angel, who went throughout the land of Egypt and slew the first-born in every home where the blood was not on the doorposts. That night at the table Peter noticed that Jesus looked sad and troubled. Turning to John, who was one of the favored disciples, he said, "Ask Him what's the matter?" John said, "Master, you look worried. Why is it?" Jesus replied: "One of you shall betray me." Peter asked, in the words of my text: "Lord, is it I?" John also asked: "Lord, is it I?" And Judas, the arch traitor, had the cheek and the audacity to look Jesus in the face and ask: "Lord, is it I?" When for days he had been bartering and bickering to betray Jesus to the Pharisees for thirty pieces of silver; or about fifteen dollars and ninety-five cents in our money.

Jesus replied: "It is he to whom I give the sop." So saying, He dipped it in the dish and handed the sop to Judas, saying: "That thou doest, do quickly." Pricked to the heart by the words of Jesus, Judas leaped to his feet, and because he was treasurer of the little apostolic band, seizing the money bag, he left the room.

And when they had sung an hymn Jesus, with the remaining eleven disciples, went out and crossed the brook Kedron and entered into the Garden of Gethsemane. This brings me to the subject of my sermon: The Three Groups in the Garden.

I. Difference in Position:

They were not grouped by their rating in Bradstreet or Dun. Every man classified himself; and you do the same. You are where you are because Jesus knows He cannot trust you in a more responsible place. Judas classified himself with the enemies of God.

The first group was near the edge of the garden; the second group farther in the garden, while Jesus, we are told, was a stone's throw farther on. The first group of disciples was so near the edge of the garden that they would have had only a short distance to go to have been outside where Judas was, with the scribes Pharisees and the mob.

I am sorry to say it, but it's the truth. The truth is not always pleasant to hear, but it's profitable for all who will profit by the truth. The first group is analogous to the position of a large percentage of members in the average church to-day. They live such a selfish, indifferent, apathetic, "good Lord, good devil," milk and chalk, cider and vinegar sort of a life that it's hard to tell whether they are in the church or in the world. I detest any man who will trim his sails to catch a passing breeze of popularity, and fight under a doubtful flag. I love to see a person come clear out for God without compromise.

The nearer the relationship the stronger are the ties of obligation. I owe to Mrs. Sunday and our children that which I do not owe to any other woman or children in the world, because of my relationship. You owe to your wife and children that which you do not owe to any other beings. I owe to Jesus that which I do not owe to the world. I testify of the world that its deeds are evil. I do not care whether they hiss me or applaud me; whether they dine me or damn me. Jesus said: "The world will hate you as it hateth Me." "Woe unto thee when all men speak well of thee." One of the most uncomplimentary things that can be said at your funeral, is that you had no enemies. If you live an uncompromising life for Christ you will have enemies.

The nearer the relationship the greater the provocation. I could in one act break my wife's heart, and bring disgrace upon my children, but that act would not put a tear in your eye. Why? Because all the interest you have toward me is that I may entertain or instruct you, and perhaps your concern ends there.

I have imagined that the conduct of multitudes who are in the church must almost break the heart of Christ. God has the right to say, "I did not send My Son into the world to bathe it in blood and tears, and open His veins with the cruel instrument of the cross, to redeem you to serve the flesh and the devil, but to serve Me. I want your influence, your time, your money, your prayers, your tears."

Alexander the Great was once asked to engage in the Olympic games. He replied: "I will, if kings are to be mine antagonists on the race track." If we were found doing nothing in this world that is not in harmony with our birth from above we would move this old sin-soaked world Godward. You cannot do as you please. The higher you climb the plainer you are seen. When you are away from home, don't forget that God is everywhere.

When the son of Fulvius was discovered with the conspirators of Catiline, his old father rebuked him by saying: "I did not beget thee to serve Catiline, but to serve your country—Rome!" You are redeemed by the precious blood of Christ, not to serve the world, but to serve God.

I love to see people as loyal to Jesus as was Speaker Lenthall to the Constitution in the days of King Charles I. When commanded to dissolve Parliament, he said: "I have neither eyes to see, ears to hear, nor tongue to speak, but as the Constitution, whose servant I am, is pleased to direct me." Or as Prince William of Orange was to the Netherlands in the thirty-seven years of war. King Philip of Spain offered him fabulous sums to surrender. Prince William sent back that message which has become mosaiced in the hearts of the Dutch people: "Not for life nor wife, nor children, nor lands would I mix in my cup one drop of the poison of treason!" No wonder, that when he was slain by the hand of an assassin, little children stopped playing and cried.

Many of our churches are not much more than mere social organizations. They spend more time in developing along social lines than along spiritual lines. Business men and influential church members do not do their duty; they are completely wrapped up in their own affairs. They are busy with the pursuits and frivolities of the world, and they lose the track. The old-time fire and the old-time spirit are lacking. What can we expect from a social club other than a leading away from God? Our churches need more of God; less of dress, strife after wealth, and social life.

A woman in a western city went to her pastor and asked: "What can I do to win my husband to Christ?" He answered: "You cannot win anyone to Christ the way you live." She hung her head in shame and went home.

When her husband and her son, a young man of eighteen, came home, she said to them: "I wish you would remain a little while after dinner. I want to speak with you." They stepped into the parlor, and she put an arm about each and said: "I have not been a consistent Christian, therefore I feel I have not been as good a wife to you, husband, or as good a mother to you, son, as I should have been. Will you join me in prayer that God will forgive me?" They all three kneeled, and she tried to pray, but all she could say was, "O God! O God!" But the Spirit broke up the fountains of the deep, and all three wept. A few days later her husband publicly accepted Christ and joined the church.

"Husband, tell me why I couldn't win you to Christ before?" she asked, and he said: "I would ask you to go with me to the theater, and you would go; to the dance, and you would go; to play cards, and you would. You drank wine with me. Then you would ask me to go to church with you, and to prayer meeting, and I would go. You went where I went, and I went where you went. You did what I did, and I did what you did. Wherein was your life any better than mine?"

To be able to convict others of sin, we must ourselves first get right with God.

II. Difference in Size:

Eight in the first group. Three in the second group. Jesus alone forms the third. The largest number in the first group. Farthest from Jesus. Nearest to the world. That has always been true of every church that I knew anything about. Ask the minister for a list of his members; then sit down and check off the prayer meeting members. You will find the largest number nearer the card party and wine supper; closer to the world than to the cross of Christ. Somebody said to Daniel Webster when he was a boy: "What are you going to be when you are a man?" "A lawyer," he replied. "But the profession is overrun." Webster answered: "There is plenty of room at the top." The nearer you get to Jesus the more elbow room you will have and the less the crowd. The most glorious exploits do not always furnish us with the clearest index of the vices or virtues of men and women. Sometimes a word, an act, a gesture; your absence or your presence will give a clearer insight into your manhood or womanhood, or lack of both, than some deed of bravery or act of prowess.

Let us talk with Jesus a minute. "Jesus, how many disciples have you?" "I had twelve. I have but eleven now." "Where is the missing one?" "He has gone to betray Me." "And yet with eleven left you are praying all alone?' Just like many a minister with hundreds of members, and bearing the burden all alone.

Judas bought a ticket for hell for thirty pieces of silver, and it wasn't a round-trip ticket either. Let us go talk with the eight:

"Where is Jesus?" "We don't know." "Where are Peter, James and John?" "Don't know; havent seen them. "Where is Judas? "Why, he just went past not long ago, with the scribes and Pharisees and a great company." "Where was he going?" "Why, he was looking for Jesus, to betray Him." "Why do you think that?" "Because to-night at the feast Jesus said, 'One of you shall betray Me, and it is he to whom I give the sop, and after dipping it in the dish He handed it to Judas." "Didn't you try to stop him in his dastardly work of betrayal?" "No." "Well, don't you suppose Judas thought he would find Jesus here with you men?"

No, he never suspected that Jesus was near that bunch. Judas knew that crowd. He knew that first group out near the edge of the garden through and through. Why do I think so? I will tell you. Jesus had gone up on the mount of transfiguration, taking with him Peter, James and John, members of the second group, and while He was away a father whose boy was possessed with a devil came to the disciples who composed the first group, out near the edge of the garden and besought them to cast the devil out of his boy.

Jesus had given His disciples power against unclean spirits, to drive them out, but instead of doing the work He gave them to do, they spent the time chewing the rag about who would be greatest in the kingdom.

I wonder if there is a father in this world who never had trouble with his boy. This father was weighed down with trouble all caused by the devil. The devil is the cause of every saloon, every drunkard, every murder, every theft, every lie, every heartache, every house of shame. All of the deception, envy, malice, filthy communications that come out of your mouth are prompted by the devil, and yet some people think I am throwing stones at them when I preach against the devil.

Some say, "Well, the devil pays, so let him stay. We need the license from the saloons to pave our streets and light our city." Yes, and you need your saloons in order to keep your jails, penitentiaries, poorhouses and insane asylums filled. Every saloon gives the devil that much better chance to get your boy.

If you want the world to be better after a while, keep the devil out of the boys and girls. If you want to drive the devil out of the world, hit him with a cradle, not a crutch.

When Jesus returned from the mount the sorrowing father ran to Him with his boy, crying, "If Thou canst do anything, have compassion on us, and help us. I brought my son to Thy disciples, and they could not cast the devil out!"

That "if" implies a doubt. Failure on the part of those disciples to keep in touch with Jesus, so they could have power to cast out devils, led the poor old father to doubt the power of Jesus. The divine philosophy, as demonstrated by thousands of church members, breeds more infidels than all the Paines, Parkers and Ingersolls combined.

As a principle increases in its meaning, it decreases in the number that should adhere to that principle. Suppose by education I mean every one who can read and write then there are about eighty-five millions of educated people in the United States. But, suppose that by education I mean every one who has graduated from high school; about one-fifth of the population would be classified as educated. On the other hand, if by education I mean every one who has graduated from a university or a college; one-half of one per cent would come under that heading.

Suppose by your friends you mean all who shake your hand, smile and say, "How are you? I am glad to see you." You have scores of friends of that sort; but suppose by friends you mean all who will stand by you through thick and thin, and defend you when they hear your name defamed, I fear they are lamentably few. Suppose by a Christian I mean every one who has his name on a church record; there are about twenty-six millions in the United States, about equally divided between the Catholics and Protestants. On the other hand, suppose I mean every man and woman who is willing to do God's will; I question whether there are ten millions that would die for Jesus.

I said to a minister one time, "How many members have you?" He said, "Eight hundred and seventy-two; but there are two hundred and seventy-eight I do not count." I asked: "Out of the number you do count, how many are helping in the meetings: singing in the choir, ushering or doing personal work?" Tears flowed down his cheeks as he said, the largest number I have been able to muster any one night was twenty-eight, and if my life depended on my making the number fifty I would die!"

There we were wearing out our lives, trying to bring that God-forsaken, whisky-soaked, gambling-cursed, harlot-blighted town to her knees, and the church calmly looking on. I sometimes doubt whether the church needs new members one-half as much as she needs the old bunch made over. Judging by the way multitudes in the church live, you would think they imagined they had a through ticket to heaven in a Pullman palace car, and had left orders for the porter to wake them up when they head into the yards of the New Jerusalem. If that's the case you will be doomed to disappointment, for you will be side-tracked with a hot box.

If I had a hundred tongues, and every tongue speaking a different language, in a different key at the same time, I could not do justice to the splendid chaos that the world-loving, dancing, card-playing, whisky-guzzling, gin-fizzling, wine-sizzling, novel-reading crowd in the church brings to the cause of Christ. There is but one voice from faithful preacher and worker about the church, and that is, "She is sick," but we say it in such painless, delicate terms that she seems to enjoy her invalidity. About four out of five who have their names on our church records are doing nothing to bring the world to Christ, and the church is not one whit better for their presence. As a satisfaction for all this, Christians are making a great deal out of Lent. I believe in a Lent that is kept three hundred and sixty-five days in the year. I think it a travesty on the teaching of Christ that any one can get such an overstock of piety on hands in forty days they can live like the devil the rest of the year. That's an old trick of the devil.

The Jewish church struck that rock and was wrecked. The Roman Catholic church struck and was split. The Protestant church is fast approaching the same doom. One of the great dangers, as I see it, it is assimilation to the world; the neglect of the poor: substitution of form for the facts of godliness; a hireling ministry, all summed up, means a fashionable church, with religion left out.

Formerly Methodists attended class meeting and gave testimony; now the class meeting has become a thing of the past. Shouts of praise used to be heard. Now such holy demonstrations are considered undignified. Occasionally some godly old sister, who is a sort of a connecting link between the old and the new, pipes up in a weak, negative falsetto, apologetic kind of a voice, and says:

"Amen, Brother Sunday!"

I don't expect one of these ossified, petrified, mildewed, dyed-in-the-wool, stamped-on-the-cork, blown-in-the-bottle, horizontal, perpendicular Presbyterians or Episcopalians to shout "Amen!" but it would do you good to loosen up. Many of you are hide-bound.

I believe half of the professing Christians amount to nothing as a spiritual force. They go to church, have a kindly regard for religion, but as for having a firm grip on God, a cheerful spirit of self-denial, enthusiastic service and prevailing prayer, and willingness to strike hard, staggering blows against the devil, they are almost failures. A shell has been invented which, when it strikes a ship, puts everybody on board to sleep. Some such thing seems to have hit our churches.

III. Difference in Revelation:

Jesus said to the members of the first group, near the edge of the garden, largest in numbers, "Sit ye here." To those composing the second, He said, "My soul is exceeding sorrowful, even unto death. Tarry ye here, and watch with Me. Watch and pray, lest ye enter into temptation. The spirit truly is willing, but the flesh is weak." But when He was alone He cried, "Father, if it be possible, let this cup pass from Me: nevertheless, not My will, but Thine, be done."

Notice the progressive stages of revelation. Not a word to Judas. To the eight nearest the world, He said, "Sit ye here." To Peter, James and John, He said, "Watch and pray." When alone with the Father, "Thy will be done." He told the Father what He did not tell Peter, James and John. He told them what He did not tell the group of eight; what He did not tell Judas. Do you wish God to reveal the deep things of the

Spirit to you? Then turn your back on the sinful things and creep close to His side.

Jesus will never unfold His revelations to you when you are lined up in front of a bar drinking, or when you are at a baseball game on the Sabbath, or living in sin. Jesus did not ask the members of the first group, near the edge of the garden, to pray. Perhaps they would have refused. Every minister knows there are certain members of his church that he never thinks of asking to lead in prayer. In fact they never darken a prayer meeting door; if a card party takes place on prayer meeting night they are at the party. Yet we wonder why this old sin-blighted world is not on her knees. I am amazed that God is doing as well as He is, with the crowd He has to work with.

Please pardon a personal reference: I was born and bred, not in Old Kentucky, although my grandfather was born in Lexington, but in Old Iowa. I was a rube of the rubes, a hayseed of the hayseeds. I have greased my hair with goose grease. I have blacked my boots with stove blacking. I have wiped my face on a gunnysack towel. I have eaten with my knife. I have drank coffee out of my saucer. I have said "done it," when I should have said, "did it;" "came," when I should have said, "come;" "seen," when I should have said, "saw." I am a graduate from the university of poverty and hard knocks, and I have taken post-graduate courses. My autobiography could be summed up in one line from Gray's "Elegy:" "The short and simple annals of the poor."

My father enlisted four months before I was born. He went to the front with Company E, Twenty-third Iowa Infantry, but he never came back. He died and was buried at Camp Patterson, Mo. I have battled my way since I was six years old. I know all about the dark and seamy side of life. If ever a man fought hard every inch of his way, I have.

One day mother said, "Boys, I am going to send you to the Soldiers' Orphans' Home at Glenwood, Iowa." We had to go to Ames to take the train. We went to a little hotel to wait, and about one o'clock some one came and said, "Get ready for the train; it's coming."

I looked into mother's face. Her eyes were red; her hair was disheveled. I said, "What's the matter, mother?" All the time Ed and I slept mother had been praying. We went to the train. Mother put one arm about me and the other about Ed, and sobbed as if her heart would break. People walked by and looked at us, but they didn't say a word. Why? They didn't know, and if they had they wouldn't have cared. Mother knew; she knew that for years she wouldn't see her boys.

We got into the train and cried, "Good-by, mother!" as the train pulled out. We reached Council Bluffs. It was cold, and we turned up our little thin coat collars over our necks and shivered. We saw a hotel, and went up and asked a woman for something to eat. She said, "What's your name?" "My name is Willie Sunday, and this is my brother Ed," I said. "Where are you going?" "Going to the Soldiers' Orphans' Home at Glenwood." She wiped her tears and said, "My husband was a soldier, and he never came back. He wouldn't turn any one away, and I certainly won't turn you boys away." She threw her arms about us and said, "Come on in." She gave us our breakfast, and our dinner too.

There wasn't any train going out on the Burlington until afternoon. We played around the yards. We saw a freight train standing there, so we climbed into the caboose. The conductor came along and said, "Where is your money?" "Ain't got any." "Where's your tickets?" "Aint got any." "You can't ride without money or tickets. I'll have to put you off."

We commenced to cry. My brother handed him a letter of introduction to the superintendent of the Orphans' Home. The conductor read it, handed it back as the tears rolled down his cheeks; then said: "Just sit still, boys. It won't cost you a cent to ride on my train." It's only twenty miles from Council Bluffs to Glenwood, and as we rounded the curve the conductor said, "There is the Home on the hill."

Mother knew. Ed didn't know. I didn't know. I went to sleep. So did Ed; but mother knew. She prayed.

Jesus knew. He prayed. Peter, James and John went to sleep. You can't make me believe that if you knew you would act as you do. If you will tell me how much you read the Bible, how much you pray, how much you do to help people to Jesus Christ, I will tell you to what figures you point on the spiritual thermometer. The trouble is, you will be in the church on Sunday morning, and will keep a little spot about eighteen inches square warm for half an hour; listen to the sermon; pick up a book and sing. "Jesus paid it all," when you have debts that are outlawed. He doesn't pay them. He doesn't pay for that hat, or that set of false teeth you are wearing. You get up and say, "I am standing on the solid rock." You are probably standing in a pair of shoes you haven't paid for yet. Let's get cleaned up for God, and see if the Lord won't do great things. He will not send the wind to drive our ships unless we have faith to lift our sails.

IV. Difference in Duty:

To the members of the first group Jesus said. "Sit ye here." To those of the second group He said, "Watch and pray." While His duty was to bear the sins of the world, there are multitudes in the church that do nothing. They are mere ciphers. At a funeral the preacher failed to appear. The undertaker thought it would be a downright shame to put the man away without something being said, and so concluded to make a few remarks himself. So when the time came he cleared his throat, and in a pious whine said: "Dear friends, this corpse has been a member of this church for forty years!"

"Crucify Him!" cried the relentless rabble. The vociferations of that infuriated mob shook the temple from foundation to turret top. Often in civil strife had been witnessed some such animosity and hatred of the multitudes. Truly all the phantoms of hell seem to have assembled in Jerusalem, and out through the funeral gate poured the mob.

Here comes Judas, leading the devil's crowd. Turning to the Pharisees, he said, "Whomsoever I shall kiss, that same is He; hold Him fast." See the smile on his hypocritical, sanctimonious countenance, as he rushes forward shouting, "Hail, Master!" and kisses Him Jesus answers, "Judas, betrayest thou the Son of man with a kiss?"

They seize Him and take Him to the High Priest's house, where He is condemned on false testimony to a felon's death on the cross.

> *"Must Jesus bear the cross alone,*
> *And all the world go free?*
> *No! There's a cross for every one,*
> *And there's a cross for me."*

As one has beautifully pictured the scene, by saying he imagined that had we been there, and God had given us power of vision, we might have seen the hilltops covered with angels, and the air filled with the heavenly hosts, all gazing breathless upon that scene. The archangel opened the door of heaven, and cried:

"O Jesus! if you want me to come to your help, raise your head and look this way; and I will come with a legion of angels to your help!" But Jesus suffered on. He imagined the archangel once more leaning over the battlements of heaven, and crying again, with a voice that shook the earth:

"O Jesus thou Son of God! If you want me to come and hurl that howling, bloodthirsty mob into hell, tear your right hand loose from the cross and wave it!" But Jesus clenched His fingers over the nails in His hands and suffered on. Why? To open up a plan of salvation which, if we will accept, will keep us out of hell.

Suddenly He cried: "It is finished!" and the Holy Spirit plucked the olive branch of peace from the cross, and winging His flight back burst through the gates of glory, shouting: "Peace! Peace! Peace! has been made through His death on the cross."

How many will go with Jesus to the last ditch? Thousands will; but there are many who, like the disciples, follow Him to the Garden, but forsake Him at the Cross. How many will say with Jesus, "Not my will, but Thine be done." Say it with me: "Not my will, but——" finish the sentence. All the peace, all the power, all the blessing of a Christian life and eternal joy are found in the three words you have left out—"Thine be done." It costs some too much to say, "Thine be done." One says, "If I say that the saloon-keepers won't come to my store to trade. If I said that I would have to close my store on the Sabbath." "If I said that I could not accept Mrs. So-and-So's invitation to a card party." "If I said that I would have to pay my debts." "If I said that I would have to go home and burn up the prizes I have won at progressive euchre." "If I said that I could not go to the brothel any more and crawl into the arms of infamy." "If I should say, 'Thy will be done.' I should have to throw the wine out of my cellar and break up my beer bottles. I am going to have a few bottles for dinner to-night." "I could not go to the ball game on Sunday afternoon if I said that." "I would have to stop lying about my neighbors if I said that." Oh, yes, it costs too much to say "Thine be done." That is the reason you lose out. That's the reason you have moral curvature of the spine. That's the reason your spiritual batting average is not up to God's league standard.

"Not my will, but—" there's where you cash in. There's where you go into the ditch. There's where you turn off the light. There's where you hang up the receiver. There's where you ring off. There's where you puncture your tire. There's where you strike out. It costs too much to say, "Thine be done."

"Say, papa, may I go with you?" asked a little boy of his father.

"Yes, son, come on," said the father, as he threw the ax over his shoulder, and, accompanied by a friend, went to the woods and felled a tree. The little fellow said:

"Say, papa, can I go and play in the water in the lagoon?"

"Yes, but be careful, and don't get into the deep water; keep close to the bank."

The little fellow was playing, digging wells, picking up stones and shells, and talking to himself, when pretty soon the father heard him cry:

"Hurry, papa, hurry!"

The father leaped to his feet, grabbed the ax and ran to the lagoon and saw the boy floundering in deep water, with hands outstretched, a look of horror on his face, as he cried:

"Hurry, papa, hurry; the alligator has got me!"

The hideous, amphibious monster had been hibernating, and had come out, lean, lank, hungry, voracious, and seized the boy. The father leaped into the lagoon and was just about to sink the ax through the head of the monster when he turned and swished the water with his huge tail like the screw of an ocean steamer, and the little fellow cried out:

"Hurry, papa, hurry!"

The blood-flecked foam told the story.

When I read that, for days I could not eat, for nights I could not sleep. I said:

"O God, what if that had been my boy!"

There are influences in this world worse than an alligator, and they are ripping and tearing to shreds our virtue, our morality. Young men are held by intemperance; others by vice. Drunkards are crying to the church, "Hurry faster!" and the church members sit on the bank playing cards, sit there drinking beer and reading novels.

"Hurry!"

They are splitting hairs over fool things, instead of trying to keep sinners out of hell!

"Faster! Faster! Faster!"

"Lord, is it I?"

Wonderful

n olden times all names meant something, and this is still the case among Indians and all other people who are living in a primitive way. Whenever you know an Indian's name and the meaning of it, you know something about the Indian. Such names as Kill Deer, Eagle Eye, Buffalo Face and Sitting Bull tell us something about the men who possessed them.

This tendency to use names that are expressive still crops out in camp life, and whenever men are thrown together in an unconventional way. In mining, military and lumber camps nearly every man has a nickname that indicates some peculiarity or trait of character. Usually a man's nickname is nearer the real man than his right name.

All of our family names to-day had their origin in something that meant something. All Bible names have a meaning, and when you read the Scriptures it will always help you to a better understanding of their meaning to look up the definition of all proper names.

There are two hundred and fifty-six names given in the Bible for the Lord Jesus Christ, and I suppose this was because He was infinitely beyond all that any one name could express.

Of the many names given to Christ it is my purpose at this time to briefly consider this one: "His name shall be called Wonderful." Let us look into it somewhat and see whether He was true to the name given Him in a prophecy eight hundred years before He was born. Does the name fit Him? Is it such a name as He ought to have?

Wonderful means something that is transcendently beyond the common; something that is away beyond the ordinary. It means something that is altogether unlike anything else. We say that Yellowstone Park, Niagara Falls and the Grand Canyon of the Colorado are wonderful because there is nothing else like them.

When David killed Goliath with his sling he did a wonderful thing, because nobody else ever did anything like it. It was wonderful that the Red Sea should open to make a highway for Israel, and wonderful that the sun should stand still for Joshua. Let us see whether Jesus was true to His name.

His birth was wonderful, for no other ever occurred that was like it. It was wonderful in that He had but one human parent, and so inherited the nature of man and the nature of God. He came to be the Prince of princes, and the King of kings, and yet His birth was not looked forward to in glad expectation, as the birth of a prince usually is in the royal palace, and celebrated with marked expressions of joy all over the country, as has repeatedly happened within the recollection of many who are here.

There was no room for Him at the inn, and He had to be born in a stable, and cradled in a manger, and yet angels proclaimed His birth with joy from the sky, to a few humble shepherds in sheepskin coats, who were watching their flocks by night.

Mark how He might have come with all the pomp and glory of the upper world. It would have been a great condescension for Him to have been born in a palace, rocked in a golden cradle and fed with golden spoons, and to have the angels come down and be His nurses. But He gave up all the glory of that world, and was born of a poor woman, and His cradle was a manger.

Think what He had come for. He had come to bless, and not to curse; to lift up, and not to cast down. He had come to seek and to save that which was lost. To give sight to the blind; to open prison doors and set captives free; to reveal the Father's love; to give rest to the weary; to be a blessing to the whole world, and yet there was no room for Him in your hearts.

His birth was also wonderful in this, that the wise men of the East were guided from far across the desert to His birthplace by a star. Nothing like this ever announced the coming of any one else into this world. As soon as His birth was known the king of the country sought His life, and ordered the slaughter of the Innocents at Bethlehem. The babies were the first Christian martyrs.

His character was wonderful, for no other has ever approached it in perfection. It is wonderful that the greatest character ever known should have come out of such obscurity, to become the most famous in all history. That such a time and such a country and such a people should have produced Jesus Christ can be accounted for on no other ground than His divinity. On his return from a trip to the Holy Land a minister was asked what had made the greatest impression upon him while there "Nazareth," he answered, and for this reason:

"The same kind of people are living there today as in the time of Jesus, and they are about the worst specimens of humanity I have seen anywhere. Lazy, lustful, ignorant and unspeakably wicked, and to think of His coming out from such a people is to me a sure proof of His divinity. Had I not been a believer in His divinity before going there, I should have to believe in it now."

His life was wonderful. Wonderful for its unselfishness, its sinlessness and its usefulness. Even His enemies could not bring against Him any graver charge than that He claimed God for His Father, and that He would do good on the Sabbath day. Not the slightest evidence of selfishness or self-interest can be found in the story of His life. He was always helping others, but not once did He do anything to help Himself. He had power to turn stones into bread, but went hungry forty days without doing it. While escaping from enemies who were determined to put Him to death He saw a man who had been blind from birth, and stopped to give him sight, doing so at the risk of His life. He never sought His own in any way, but lived for others every day of His life. His first miracle was performed, not before a multitude to spread His own fame, but in a far-away hamlet, to save a peasant's wife from humiliation. He had compassion on the hungry multitude and wept over Jerusalem, but He never had any mercy on Himself.

His teaching was wonderful. It was wonderful for the way in which He taught; for its simplicity and clearness, and adaptation to the individual. Nowhere do you find Him seeking the multitude, but He never avoided the individual. And His teaching was always adapted to the comprehension of those whom He taught. It is said that the common people heard Him gladly, and this shows that they understood what He said. He put the cookies on the lower shelf. No man had to take a dictionary with him when he went to hear the Sermon on the Mount. He illustrated His thought and made plain His meaning by the most wonderful word-pictures. The preacher who would reach the people must have something to say, and know how to say it so that those who hear will know just what he means.

Jesus made His meaning clear by using plenty of illustrations. He didn't care a rap what the scribes and Pharisees thought about it, or said about it. He wanted the people to know what He meant, and that is why He was always so interesting. The preacher who can't make his preaching interesting has no business in the pulpit. If he can't talk over ten minutes without making people begin to snap their watches and go to yawning all over the house, he has misunderstood the Lord about his call to preach. Jesus was interesting because He could put the truth before people in an interesting way. We are told that without a parable He spake not to any man. He made people see things, and see them clearly. It is wonderful that this humble Galilean peasant, who may never have gone to school a day in His life, should have made Himself a Teacher of teachers for all time. The pedagogy of to-day is modeling after the manner of Christ closer and closer every day.

He was wonderful in His originality. The originality of Jesus is a proof of His divinity. The human mind cannot create anything in an absolute sense. It can build out of almost any kind of material, but it cannot create. There is no such thing as out-and-out originality belonging to man. You cannot imagine anything that does not resemble something you have previously seen or heard of.

I grant that you can take a cow and a horse and a dog and a sheep and from them make animals enough to fill Noah's ark, but you must have the cow and the horse and the dog and the sheep for a beginning. Everything you make will simply be a modification of the various forms and properties of them.

There is said to be nothing new under the sun, and there is a sense in which it is true. Everything is the outgrowth of something else. The first railway cars looked like the old stage-coaches, and the first automobiles looked like carriages. It is that way about everything. No man ever made a book, or even a story, that was altogether unlike all others.

The stories we hear to-day on the Irish and Dutch are older than the Irish and Dutch. You can find stories like them in the earliest literature, but you can't find any stories anywhere in any literature that even in the remotest way resemble the parables of Jesus. Such parables as the prodigal son and the Good Samaritan are absolutely new creations, and so proclaim Jesus as divine, because He could create.

His teaching was wonderful, not only in the way He taught, but in what He taught. He taught that He was greater than Moses. Think of the audacity of it! Making such claims as that to the Jews, who regarded Moses as being almost divine. Think of the audacity of some man of obscure and humble parentage standing before us Americans and trying to make us think he was greater than George Washington.

Jesus also declared that He fulfilled the prophecies and the law of Moses, and the only effort He ever made to prove His claim was to point to the works that He did. The first thing an impostor always does is to overprove his case. Jesus never turned His hand over to try to convince His enemies that He was the Christ. You have to explain a coal-oil lamp, but you don't need to waste any breath in giving information about the power of the sun. The springtime will do that by making all nature burst into bud, flower and leaf, and the power of Christ is shown just as convincingly in the changed lives of men and women who believe in Him.

Jesus taught that all would be lost who did not believe on Him. I have seen multitudes of saved people, but I have yet to see one who did not get his salvation by believing on Christ. Find the place in this world that comes the nearest to being like hell itself, and you will find it filled with those who are haters of Jesus Christ. You can't argue it. Go into saloons, gambling hells, and such places, and the people you find there are all haters of Jesus Christ, and the more of them you find the more the place in which you find them will be like hell itself.

Jesus taught that He was equal to God. He said, "He that hateth Me hateth My Father also" (John 15:23). Did you ever know of anybody else making such claims? He said, "Come unto me, all ye that labor and are heavy laden, and I will give you rest." Offering to bear the burden of the whole world. Think of it! He said, "I am come that they might have life, and that they might have it more abundantly." And He said, "I am the resurrection and the life; and he that believeth in Me, though he were dead, yet shall he live. And whosoever liveth and believeth in Me shall never die." Surely He was wonderful in what He taught.

It is not surprising that He so stirred them in the Capernaum synagogue, where He taught them not as the scribes, but as one having authority. Is it any wonder that they were right after Him for heresy? Let any one to-day begin to teach in our churches something as entirely new as the teachings of Jesus were, and see what will happen.

He was wonderful in what He prophesied of Himself. He foretold how He would die, and when He would die. It was wonderful that He should have been betrayed into the hands of those who sought His life, by one of His own trusted disciples, and wonderful that He should have been sold for so low a price.

Wonderful, too, that He should have been condemned to death in the way in which He was, by both the religious and civil authorities, and on the testimony of false witnesses, in the name of God, when all the laws of God were defied in the trial. It was wonderful that He was tormented and tortured so cruelly before being sent to the cross, and that He should have been put to death in the brutal manner in which He was. The time of His death was also wonderful; on the day of the Passover, thus Himself becoming the real Passover, to which the passover lamb had so long pointed.

The great publicity of His death was also wonderful. It is doubtful if any other death was ever witnessed by so many people. Hundreds of thousands of people were in Jerusalem, who had come from everywhere to attend the Passover. The sky was darkened, and the sun hid his face from the awful scene. A great earthquake shook the city; the dead came out of their graves, and went into the city, appearing unto many, and the veil of the temple was rent from top to bottom. And remember that up to that time no eye had been allowed to look behind that veil, except that of the high priest, and then only once a year, on the great Day of Atonement.

His resurrection was wonderful. He had foretold it to His disciples, and had done so frequently, always saying, whenever He spoke of His death, that He would rise again on the third day, and yet every one of them appeared to forget all about it, and not one of them was expecting it. None of them thought of going to the sepulcher on the morning of the third day, except the women, and they only to prepare His body more fully for the grave. Womanhood has always been on the firing line.

This shows how fully they had abandoned all hope when they saw Him dead. Some left the city, for we are told of two who went to Emmaus. The manner of His resurrection was godlike. No human mind could ever have imagined such a scene. Had some man described it in the way in which he thought it should have occurred, he would have had earthquakes and thunders and a great commotion in the heavens. A sound like that of the last trump would have proclaimed to all the terrified inhabitants of Jerusalem that He was risen. But see how far different it was.

An angel rolled away the stone from the mouth of the sepulcher as quietly as the opening of the buds in May, and the women, who were early there, found no disorder in the grave, but the linen clothes with which they had tenderly robed His body were neatly folded and tidily placed.

And then how wonderful are the recorded appearances after the resurrection, again so different from what man would have had them. He appeared to every one if His friends, and to His best friends, but not a single one of His enemies got to see Him. I know that this story of the resurrection is true, because none but God would have had things happen in the order that they did, and in the way in which they occurred. Had the story been false the record would have made Jesus go to Pilate and the high priest, and to the others who had put Him to death, to prove that He was risen.

The effect of His teaching upon the world has been wonderful. Remember that He left no great colleges to promulgate His doctrines, but committed them to a few humble fishermen, whose names are now the most illustrious in all history. Looked at from the human side alone, how great was the probability that everything He had said would be forgotten within a few years. He never wrote a sermon. He published no books. Not a thing He said was engraved upon stone or scrolled upon brass, and yet His doctrines have endured for two thousand years. They have gone to the ends of the earth, and have wrought miracles wherever they have gone. They have lifted nations out of darkness and degradation and sin, and have made the wilderness to blossom as the rose.

When Jesus began His ministry Rome ruled the world, and her invincible legions were everywhere, but now through the teachings of the humble Galilean peasant, whom her minions put to death, her power and her religion are gone. The great temple of Diana of the Ephesians is in ruins, and no worshipper of her can be found.

When Jesus fed the five thousand with a few loaves and fishes, and healed the poor woman who touched the hem of His garment, there wasn't a church, or a hospital, or an insane asylum, or other eleemosynary institution in the world, and now they are nearly as countless as the sands upon the seashore. When the bright cloud hid Him from the gaze of those who loved Him with a devotion that took them to martyrdom, the only record of His sayings was graven upon their hearts, but now libraries are devoted to the consideration of them. No words were ever so weighty or so weighed as those of Him who was so poor that He had not where to lay His head. The scholarship of the world has sat at His feet with bared head, and has been compelled to say again and again, "Never man spake as He spake." His utterances have been translated into every known tongue, and have carried healing on their wings wherever they have gone. No other book has ever had a tithe of the circulation of that which contains His words, and not only that, but His thoughts and the story of His life are so interwoven in all literature that if a man should never read a line in the Bible, and yet be a reader at all he could not remain ignorant of the Christ.

He is true to His name because He is a wonderful Savior now. You have only to lift your eyes and look about you to see that His wonderful salvation is going on everywhere to-day. This vast audience throws the lie back into your teeth when you say the religion of Jesus Christ is dying out. There has never been a time when the love of Christ gripped the hearts of humanity as it does to-day.

When John the Baptist, in prison, sent two of his disciples to Jesus, saying: "Art thou He that should come, or do we look for another?" Jesus sent this answer to John: "The blind receive their sight; the lame walk, the lepers are cleansed, and the deaf hear; the dead are raised up, and the poor have the gospel preached unto them"; and that test of His power is as apparent in nearly every part of the world to-day as it was in Galilee. If you have eyes to see the works of God, you will always find them going on. The heavens declare the glory of God, but there are people so blind they can't see anything but a spell of weather in the rainbow.

Jerry McAuley in prison, a man who had lived by crime, and who had never heard the name of God outside of profanity; as blind and and dead to anything good as a stone, one Sunday in the prison chapel heard a verse of Scripture quoted that took hold of his attention. He thought he would like to see it and read it for himself. So he took the Bible in his cell and began to search for it. He didn't know but one sure way to find it, and that was to begin at the first verse in the Bible and read straight on until he came to it. The verse he wanted was in Hebrews, away over in the back part of the New Testament.

Jerry read on, chapter after chapter, and day after day, looking for that verse, but long before he found it he found Jesus Christ—just as some of you would do if you would only be honest with God, and give Him a chance at you by reading His word. From that time on everybody who came near Jerry McAuley knew that the eyes of the man born blind had been opened in him. He started the Water Street Mission in New York, where I don't believe a service was ever held in which somebody was not converted.

Any number of men who were headed straight for the devil are preaching the gospel to-day because they were stopped by the light of God and the voice of His Christ as suddenly at St. Paul was. Yes, He is a wonderful Savior because He is able to save the uttermost now.

A man would be a great surgeon who could save ninety per cent of those upon whom he operated, but mark this: Jesus Christ never lost a case. He never found a case that was too hard for Him. His disciples were continually finding cases they thought were hopeless, and this shows how little they knew Him while He was with them.

Jesus never sent anybody away who came honestly and earnestly seeking His help. They brought to Him all kinds of desperate cases, but at a word or a touch from Him their troubles were all gone. The hardest cases were no more difficult for Him than the easiest, and the same is true to-day for there is no change in Him. He is the same yesterday, to-day and forever. He can save the scarlet sinner—the man who commits murder—as easily as He can the woman who cheats at cards.

He is a wonderful Savior, too, because He can save so quickly. Quicker than thought He can give you life. It is only, look and live. As quick as you can come He receives you, and as quickly as you could receive a present you had been wanting for years, you can have salvation "Him that cometh to Me I will in nowise cast out." "To as many as received Him, to them gave He power to become the sons of God." No need of taking very much time about that.

In a meeting Thomas Harrison was holding, a railroad engineer came forward with his watch in his hand and said, "Mr. Harrison, can

I be saved in ten minutes? I must leave here to take my train out then."

"Yes," replied Harrison, "you can be saved in ten seconds." The man dropped on his knees, was quickly saved and had seven minutes to spare. A conductor on a fast Pennsylvania train, in Ohio, was converted while crossing a bridge fifty feet long, when going at the rate of a mile a minute. Yes, indeed, He is a wonderful Savior because He can save so quickly.

Moody used to tell of a banker in San Francisco, who was awakened in the night by a burglar at his bedside. The robber held a revolver almost against his face, and said, "If you move I'll kill you!" The banker said, "God have mercy on my soul!" and knocked the burglar down before he could pull the trigger, and was soundly converted before the man struck the floor, as his life afterward proved.

And now I come to the last evidence I will give you that He is true to His name, and that is—

He is a wonderful Savior because He saved me. There is nothing that can be so convincing to a man as his own experience. I do not know that I am the son of my mother any more certainly than I know that I am a child of God, and I do not know that I have been born in a natural way any more convincingly than I know that I have been born of the Spirit.

And now let me ask you this: Has this wonderful Savior saved you? Do you know Him as your Savior? Have you ever given Him your case? When the proof is so overwhelming that He does save, and has been saving for centuries, and that none have ever been saved or ever can be saved except through Him, is it not wonderful that any one can be indifferent to the claims of Jesus Christ?

What Shall the End Be

No book ever came by luck or chance. Every book owes its existence to some being or beings, and within the range and scope of human intelligence there are but three things —good, bad and God. All that originates in intellect; all which the intellect can comprehend, must come from one of the three. This book, the Bible, could not possibly be the product of evil, wicked, godless, corrupt, vile men, for it pronounces the heaviest penalties against sin. Like produces like, and if bad men were writing the Bible they never would have pronounced condemnation and punishment against wrong-doing. So that is pushed aside.

The holy men of old, we are told, spake as they were moved by the Holy Ghost. Men do not attribute these beautiful and matchless and well-arranged sentences to human intelligence alone, but we are told that men spake as they were inspired by the Holy Ghost.

The only being left, to whom you, or I or any sensible person could ascribe the origin of the Bible, is God, for here is a book, the excellence of which rises above other books, like mountains above molehills—a book whose brilliancy and life-giving power exceed the accumulated knowledge and combined efforts of men, as the sun exceeds the lamp, which is but a base imitation of the sun's glory. Here is a book that tells me where I came from and where I am going, a book without which I would not know of my origin or destiny, except as I might glean it from the dim outlines of reason or nature, either or both of which would be unsatisfactory to me. Here is a book that tells me what to do and what not to do.

Most men believe in God. Now and then you find a man who doesn't, and he's a fool, for "The fool hath said in his heart, there is no

God." Most men have sense. Occasionally you will find a fool, or an infidel, who doesn't believe in God. Most men believe in a God that will reward the right and punish the wrong; therefore it is clear what attitude you ought to assume toward my message tonight, for the message I bring to you is not from human reason or intelligence, but from God's Book.

"What shall the end be of them that obey not the gospel of God?" Now listen, and I will try to help you. Israel's condition was desperate. Peter told them that if they continued to break God's law, they would merit his wrath. I can imagine him crying out in the words of Jeremiah: "What will you do in the swelling of the Jordan?" I hear him cry in the words of Solomon: "The way of the transgressor is hard." That seems to have moved him, and I can hear him cry in the words of my text: "What shall the end be of them that obey not the gospel of God?"

There are those who did obey. Peter knew what their end would be—blessings here and eternal life hereafter—but he said, "What shall the end be of them that obey not?"

A man said, "I cannot be a Christian. I cannot obey God." That is not true. That would make God out a demon and a wretch. God says if you are not a Christian you will be doomed. If God asked mankind to do something, and he knew when he asked them that they could not do it, and he told them he would damn them if they didn't do it, it would make God out a demon and a wretch, and I will not allow you or any other man to stand up and insult my God. You can be a Christian if you want to, and it is your cussedness that you are unwilling to give up that keeps you away from God.

Supposing I should go on top of a building and say to my little baby boy, "Fly up to me." If he could talk, he would say, "I can't." And supposing I would say, "But you can; if you don't I'll whip you to death." When I asked him to do it, I knew he couldn't, yet I told him I would whip him to death if he didn't, and in saying that I would, as an earthly father, be just as reasonable as God would be if he should ask you to do something you couldn't do, and though he knew when he asked you that you couldn't do it, nevertheless would damn you if you didn't do it.

Don't tell God you can't. Just say you don't want to be a Christian, that's the way to be a man. Just say, "I don't want to be decent; I don't want to quit cussing; I don't want to quit booze-fighting; I don't want to quit lying; I don't want to quit committing adultery. If I should be a Christian I would have to quit all these things, and I don't want to do it." Tell God you are not man enough to be a Christian. Don't try to saddle it off on the Lord. You don't want to do it, that's all; that's the trouble with you.

A man in a town in Ohio came and handed one of the ministers a letter, and he said, "I want you to read that when you get home." When the minister got home he opened it and it read like this:

"I was at the meeting last night, and somehow or other the words 'What shall the end be?' got hold of me, and troubled me. I went to bed, but couldn't sleep. I got up and went to my library. I took down my books on infidelity and searched them through and searched through the writings of Voltaire, and Darwin, and Spencer, and Strauss, and Huxley, and Tyndall, and through the lectures of Ingersoll, but none of them could answer the cry and longing of my heart, and I turn to you. Is there help? Where will I find it?" And that man found it where every man ever has, or ever will find it, down at the Cross of Jesus Christ, and I have been praying God that might be the experience of many a man and woman in this Tabernacle.

Ever since God saved my soul and sent me out to preach, I have prayed him to enable me to pronounce two words, and put into those words all they will mean to you; if they ever become a reality, God pity you. One word is "Lost," and the other is "Eternity."

Ten thousand years from now we will all be somewhere. Ten thousand times ten thousand times ten thousand years, the eternity has just begun. Increase the multiple and you will only increase the truth. If God should commission a bird to carry this earth, particle by particle, to yonder planet, making a round trip once in a thousand years, and if, after the bird had performed that task God should prolong its life, and it would carry the world back, particle by particle, making a round trip once in a thousand years, and put everything back as it was originally, after it had accomplished its task, you would have been five minutes in eternity; and yet you sit there with just a heart-beat between you and the judgment of God. I have been praying that God would enable me to pronounce those two words and put in them all they will mean to you, that I might startle you from your lethargy. I prayed God, too, that he might give me some new figure of speech tonight, that he might impress my mind, that I, in turn, might impress your mind in such a manner that I could startle you from your indifference and sin, until you would rush to Jesus.

What is your life? A hand's breadth—yes, a hair's breadth—yes, one single heart-beat, and you are gone, and yet you sit with the judgment of God hovering over you. "What shall the end be?"

I never met any man or woman in my life who disbelieved in Christianity but could not be classified under one of these two headings.

First—They who, because of an utter disregard of God's claims upon their lives, have, by and through that disregard, become poltroons, marplots or degenerate scoundrels, and have thrown themselves beyond the pale of God's mercy.

Second—Men and women with splendid, noble and magnificent abilities, which they have allowed to become absorbed in other matters, and they do not give to the subjects of religion so much as passing attention. They have the audacity to claim for themselves an intellectual superiority to those who believe the Bible, which they sneeringly term "that supersition." But, listen! I will challenge you. If you will bring to religion or to the divinity of Jesus, or the salvation of your soul, the same honest inquiry you demand of yourself in other matters, you will know God is God; you will know the Bible is the Word of God, and you will know Jesus Christ is the Son of God. You will know that you are a sinner on the road to hell, and you will turn from your sins. But you don't give to religion, you don't demand of yourself, the same amount of research that you would demand of yourself if you were going to buy a piece of property, to find out whether or not the title was perfect. You wouldn't buy it if you didn't know the title was without a flaw, and yet you will pass the Bible by and claim you have more sense than the person who does investigate and finds out, accepts and is saved.

What is the Gospel that the people ought to obey it? It is good news, glad tidings of salvation, through Jesus Christ.

Oh, but somebody says, do you call the news of that book that I am on the road to hell, good news? No sir; that in itself is not good news, but since it is the truth, the sooner you find out the better it will be for you.

Supposing you are wandering, lost in a swamp, and a man would come to you and say: "You are lost." That wouldn't help you. But supposing the man said: "You are lost; I am a guide; I know the way out. If you put yourself in my care, I will lead you back to your home, back to your loved ones." That would meet your condition.

Now God doesn't tell you that you are lost, and on the road to hell, and then leave you, but he tells you that you are on the road to hell, and he says, "I have sent a guide, my Son, to lead you out, and to lead you back to peace and salvation." That's good news, that God is kind enough to tell you that you are lost, and on the road to hell, and that he sends a guide, who, if you will submit, will lead you out of your condition and lead you to peace and salvation. That's gospel; that's good news that tells a man that he needn't go to hell unless he wants to.

When the Israelites were bitten by the serpents in the wilderness, wasn't it good news for them to know that Moses had raised up a brazen serpent and bid them all to look and be healed?

When the flood came, wasn't it good news for Noah to know that he would be saved in the ark?

When the city of Jericho was going to fall, wasn't it good news to Rahab. She had been kind and had hid two of God's servants who were being pursued as spies. They were running across the housetops to get away to the wall to drop down, and Rahab covered them, on top of her house, with grass and corn, and when the men came they could not find them. After the men had gone, Rahab gave them cord and lowered them down the wall, and God said to her, "Because you did that for my servants, I will save you and your household when I take the city of Jericho. What I want you to do is to hang a scarlet line out of window and I will save all that are under your roof." Wasn't it good news to her to know that she and all her household would be saved by hanging a scarlet line out of the window? Never has such news been published. "Thou shalt call his name Jesus, for he shall save his people from their sins." It was good news, but never has such news reached the world as that man need not go to hell, for God has provided redemption for them that will accept of it and be saved.

Supposing a man owed you $5,000 and he had nothing to pay it with. You would seize him and put him in jail, and supposing while there, your own son would come and say: "Father, how much does he owe you?" "Five thousand dollars." And your son would pay it and the man would be released.

Ah, my friends, hear me! We were all mortgaged to God, had nothing with which to pay, and inflexible justice seized upon us and put us in the prison of condemnation. God took pity on us. He looked around to find some one to pay our debts. Jesus Christ stepped forward and said: "I'll go; I'll become bone of their bone and flesh of their flesh." God gave man the Mosaic law. Man broke the law. .

If a Jew violated the law he was compelled to bring a turtle dove, or pigeon, or heifer, or bullock to the high priest for a sacrifice, and the shedding of its blood made atonement for his sins. Once a year the high priest would kill the sacrifice, putting it on the altar. That made atonement for the sins of the people during the year. Then they would put their hands on the head of the scape-goat, and lead it out into the wilderness.

Jesus Christ came into the world, born of a woman. When he shed his blood, he made atonement for our sins. God says, "If you will accept Jesus Christ as your Saviour, I will put it to your credit as though you kept the law." And it's Jesus Christ or hell for every man or woman on God Almighty's dirt. There is no other way whereby you can be saved. It's good news that you don't have to go to hell, unless you want to.

When the North German Lloyd steamer, the *Elbe*, went down in the North Sea, years and years ago, only nineteen of her passengers and crew were saved. Among them was a county commissioner who lived in Cleveland, Ohio, and when he reached the little English town he sent a cablegram to his wife, in which he said, "The *Elbe* is lost; I am saved." She crumpled that cablegram, ran down the street to her neighbors, and as she ran she waved it above her head and cried, "He's saved! He's saved!" That cablegram is framed, and hangs upon the walls of their beautiful Euclid Avenue home. It was good news to her that he whom she loved was saved.

Good news I bring you. Good news I bring you, people. You need not go to hell if you will accept the Christ that I preach to you.

"What shall the end be of them that obey not the gospel?" And the gospel of God is, "Repent or you will go to hell." "What shall the end be of them that obey not the gospel?" We have seen that it is good news; now what is it to obey? What was it for Israel to obey? Look at the brazen serpent on the pole. What was it for Noah to obey? Build the ark and get into it. What was it for Rahab to obey? Hang a scarlet line out of the window, and God would pass her by when he took the city of Jericho. All that was obeying. It was believing God's message and obeying.

Ah! I see a man. He walks to the banks of the Seine, in Paris, to end his life. He walked to the bank four times, but he didn't plunge in. He filled a cup with poison, three times raised it to his lips, but he did not drink. He cocked the pistol, put it against his temple. He did that twice, but he didn't pull the trigger. He heard the story of Jesus Christ and dropped on his knees, and William Cowper wrote:

> "God moves in a mysterious way,
> His wonders to perform;
> He plants his footsteps in the sea,
> And rides upon the storm.
>
> "There is a fountain filled with blood,
> Drawn from Immanuel's veins;
> And sinners plunged beneath that flood,
> Lose all their guilty strains."

So that's what you found, is it, Cowper?

I go to Bridgeport, Connecticut. I rap at a humble home and walk into the presence of Fanny J. Crosby, the blind hymn-writer. She has written over six thousand hymns. She never saw the light of day, was born blind, and I say to her, "Oh, Miss Crosby, tell me that I may tell the people what you have found by trusting in the finished work of Jesus Christ? You have sat in darkness for ninety-four years; tell me, Miss Crosby." And that face lights up like a halo of glory; those sightless eyes flash, and she cries:

> "Blessed assurance, Jesus is mine;
> Oh, what a foretaste of glory divine!"

"Pass me not, O gentle Saviour,
Hear my humble cry!"

"Jesus keep me near the cross,
There's a precious fountain."

"Once I was blind, but now I can see,
The light of the world is Jesus."

"And I shall see Him, face to face,
And tell the story, Saved by Grace."

I go to Wesley as he walks along the banks of a stream, while the storm raged, the lightning flashed and the thunder roared. The birds were driven, in fright, from their refuge in the boughs of the trees. A little bird took refuge in his coat. Wesley held it tenderly, walked home, put it in a cage, kept it until morning, carried it out, opened the door and watched it as it circled around and shot off for its mountain home. He returned to his house and wrote:

"Jesus, lover of my soul,
Let me to thy bosom fly."

What have you found by trusting in the finished work of Jesus Christ?

It is said of Napoleon that one day he was riding in review before his troops, when the horse upon which he sat became unmanageable, seized the bit in his teeth, dashed down the road and the life of the famous warrior was in danger. A private, at the risk of his life, leaped out and seized the runaway horse, while Napoleon, out of gratitude, raised in the stirrups, saluted and said, "Thank you, captain." The man said, "Captain of what, sir?" "Captain of my Life Guards, sir," said he.

The man stepped over to where the Life Guards were in consultation and they ordered him back into the ranks. He refused to go and issued orders to the officer by saying, "I am Captain of the Guards." Thinking him insane, they ordered his arrest and were dragging him away, when Napoleon rode up and the man said, "I am Captain of the Guards because the Emperor said so." And Napoleon arose and said, "Yes, Captain of my Life Guards. Loose him, sir; loose him."

I am a Christian because God says so, and I did what he told me to do, and I stand on God's Word and if that book goes down, I'll go down with it. If God goes down, I'll go with him, and if there were any other kind of God, except that God, I would have been shipwrecked long ago. Twenty-seven years ago in Chicago I piled all I had, my reputation, my character, my wife, children, home; I staked my soul, everything I had, on the God of that Bible, and the Christ of that Bible, and I won.

"What shall the end be of them that obey not the gospel of God?" Hear me! There are three incomprehensibilities to me. Don't think there are only three things I don't know, or don't you think that I think there are only three things I don't know. I say, there are three things that I cannot comprehend.

First—Eternity; that something away off yonder, somewhere. You will think it will end. It leads on, on, on and on. I can take a billion, I can subtract a million; I can take a million or a billion, or a quadrillion, or a septillion of years from eternity, and I haven't as much as disturbed its original terms. Minds trained to deal with intricate problems will go reeling back in their utter inability to comprehend eternity.

And there is space. When you go out tonight, look up at the moon, 240,000 miles away. Walking forty miles a day, I could reach the moon in seventeen years, but the moon is one of our near neighbors. Ah, you saw the sun today, 92,900,000 miles away. I couldn't walk to the sun. If I could charter a fast train, going fifty miles an hour, it would take the train two hundred and fifteen years to reach the sun.

In the early morn you will see a star, near the sun—Mercury—91,000,000 miles away; travels around the sun once in eighty-eight days, going at the speed of 110,000 miles an hour, as it swings in its orbit.

Next is Venus; she is beautiful; 160,000,000 miles away, travels around the sun once in 224 days, going at the rate of 79,000 miles an hour, as she swings in her orbit.

Then comes the earth, the planet upon which we live, and as you sit there, this old earth travels around the sun, once in 365 days, or one calendar year, going at the speed of 68,000 miles an hour, and as you sit there and I stand here, this old planet is swinging in her orbit 68,000 miles an hour, and she is whirling on her axis nineteen miles a second. By force of gravity we are held from falling into illimitable space.

Yonder is Mars, 260,000,000 miles away. Travels around the sun once in 687 days, or about two years, going at the speed of 49,000 miles an hour. Who knows but that it is inhabited by a race unsullied by sin, untouched by death?

Yonder another, old Jupiter, champion of the skies, sashed and belted around with vapors of light. Jupiter, 480,000,000 miles away, travels around the sun once in twelve years, going at the speed of 30,000 miles an hour. I need something faster than an express train, going fifty miles an hour, or a cyclone, going one hundred miles an hour. If I could charter a Pullman palace car and couple it to a ray of light, which travels at the speed of 192,000 miles a second—if I could attach my Pullman palace car to a ray of light, I could go to Jupiter and get back tomorrow morning for breakfast at nine o'clock, but Jupiter is one of our near neighbors.

Yonder is old Saturn, 885,000,000 miles away. Travels around the sun once in twenty years, going at the speed of 21,000 miles an hour.

Away yonder, I catch a faint glimmer of another stupendous world, as it swings in its tireless and prodigious journey. Old Uranus, 1,780,000,000 miles away. Travels around the sun once in eighty-four years, going at the speed of two hundred and fifty miles an hour.

As the distance of the planets from the sun increases, their velocity in their orbit correspondingly decreases.

I say is that all? I hurry to Chicago and take the Northwestern. I rush out to Lake Geneva, Wisconsin, I climb into the Yerkes observatory, and I turn the most ponderous telescope in the world to the skies, and away out on the frontier of the universe, on the very outer rim of the world, I catch a faint glimmer of Neptune, 2,790,000,000 miles away. Travels round the sun once in one hundred and sixty-four years, going at the speed of two hundred and ten miles an hour. If I could step on the deck of a battleship and aim a 13-inch gun, and that projectile will travel 1,500 miles in a minute, it would take it three hundred and sixty years to reach that planet.

Away out yonder is Alpha Centauri. If I would attach my palace car to a ray of light and go at the speed of 192,000 miles a second, it would take me three years to reach that planet. An express train, going thirty miles an hour, would be 80,000,000 years pulling into Union depot at Alpha Centauri.

Yonder, the Polar or the North star. Traveling at a rate of speed of 192,000 miles a second, it would take me forty-five years to reach that planet. And if I would go to the depot and buy a railroad ticket to the North star, and pay three cents a mile, it would cost me $72,000,000 for railroad fare to go to that planet.

"Oh, God, what is man, that thou art mindful of him?" And the fool, the fool, the fool hath said in his heart, "There is no God." I'm not an infidel, because I am no fool. "The Heavens declare the glory of God and the firmament showeth his handiwork." I don't believe an infidel ever looked through a telescope or studied astronomy.

"What is man, that thou are mindful of him?" These are days when it is "Big man, little God." These are days when it is gigantic "I," and pigmy "God." These are days when it is "Ponderous man, infinitestimal God."

There are 1,400,000,000 people on earth. You are one of that number, so am I. None of us amount to much. What do you or I amount to out of 1,400,000,000 people? If I could take an auger and bore a hole in the top of the sun, I could pour into the sun 1,400,000,000 worlds the size of the planet upon which we live, and there would be room in the sun for more. Then think of the world, and God made that world, the God that you cuss, the God that wants to keep you out of hell, the God whose Son you have trampled beneath your feet.

If you take 1,400,000,000, multiply it by 1,400,000,000, multiply that by 1,000,000, multiply that by millions, multiply that by infinity, that's God. If you take 1,400,000,000 subtract 1,400,000,000, subtract millions, subtract, subtract, subtract, subtract on down, that's you. If ever a man appears like a consummate ass and an idiot, it's when he says he don't believe in a God or tries to tell God his plan of redemption don't appeal to him.

And the third: The third is the love of God to a lost and sin-cursed world and man's indifference to God's love. How he has trampled God's love beneath his feet, I don't understand. I don't understand why you have grown gray-haired, and are not a Christian. I don't understand why you know right from wrong, and still are not a Christian. I don't understand it. Listen! What is it to obey the Gospel? The Gospel is good news, and to obey it is to believe in Jesus. What is it not to obey? What was the end of those who weren't in the ark with Noah? They found a watery grave. What was the end of those who didn't look at the brazen serpent in the wilderness? They died. What was the end of those who were not with Rahab when she hung out the scarlet line? They perished.

When a man starts on a journey he has one object in view—the end. A journey is well, if it ends well. We are all on a journey to eternity. What will be the end? My text doesn't talk about the present. Your present is, or may be, an enviable position in church, club life, or commercial life, lodge, politics; your presence may be sought after to grace every social gathering. God doesn't care about that. What shall the end be? When all that is gone, when pleasures pass away, and sorrow and weeping and wailing take their place, what shall the end be?

Some people deny that their suffering in the other world will be eternal fire. Do you think your scoffs can extinguish the flames of hell? Do you think you can annihilate hell because you don't believe in it? We have a few people who say, "Matter is non-existent," but that doesn't do away with the fact that matter is existent, just because we have some people who haven't sense enough to see it. You say, "I don't believe there is a hell." Well, there is, whether you believe it or not. You say, "I don't believe Jesus Christ is the Son of God." Well, he is, whether you believe it or not. Some people say, "I don't believe there is a heaven." There is, whether you believe it or not. You say, "I don't believe the Bible is the Word of God." Well, it is, and your disbelief does not change the fact, and the sooner you wake up to that the better for you. I might say that I don't believe George Washington ever lived. I never saw him, but it wouldn't do away with the fact that he did live, and George Washington lies buried on the banks of the Potomac. You say you don't believe there is a hell, but that doesn't do away with the fact that there is a hell.

What difference does it make whether the fire in hell is literal, or the fittest emblem God could employ to describe to us the terrible punishment? Do you believe the streets of heaven are paved with literal gold? Do you believe that? When we talk about gold we all have high and exalted ideas. How do you know but that God said "streets of gold" in order to convey to us the highest ideal our minds could conceive of beauty? It doesn't make any difference whether the gold on the streets in heaven is literal or not. What difference does it make whether the fire in hell is literal or not? When we talk about fire everybody shrinks from it. Suppose God used that term as figurative to convey to you the terror of hell. You are a fool to test the reality of it. It must be an awful place if God loved us well enough to give Jesus to keep us out of there. I don't want to go there.

I said to a fellow one time, "Don't you think that possibly there is a hell?"

He said, "Well, yes, possibly there may be a hell."

I said, "It's pretty good sense, then, to get ready for the maybe." Well, just suppose there is a hell. It's good sense to get ready, them, even for the "maybe." I don't look like a man that would die very quickly, do I? I have just as good a physique as you ever gazed at. I wouldn't trade with any man I know. A lot of you fellows are stronger than I, but I have as a good a physique as ever you looked at. I have been preaching at this pace for fourteen years, and I've stood it, although I begin to feel myself failing a little bit. But I don't look like a man who would die quickly, do I? But I may die, and on that possibility I carry thousands of dollars of life insurance. I don't believe that any man does right to himself, his wife or his children if he doesn't provide for them with life insurance, so when he is gone they will not be thrown upon the charity of the world. And next to my faith, if I should die tonight, that which would give me the most comfort would be the knowledge that I have in a safe deposit vault in Chicago life insurance papers, paid up to date, and my wife could cash in and she and the babies could listen to the wolves howl for a good many years. I don't expect to die soon, but I may die, and on that "may" I carry thousands of dollars in life insurance.

I take a train to go home, I don't expect the train to be wrecked, but it may be wrecked, and on that "maybe" I carry $10,000 a year in an accident policy. It may go in the ditch. That's good sense to get ready for the "maybe." Are you a business man? Do you carry insurance on your stock? Yes. On the building? Yes. Do you expect it to burn? No, sir. But it may burn, so you are ready for it. Every ship is compelled, by law, to carry life-preservers and life-boats equal to the passenger capacity. They don't expect the ship to sink, but it may sink and they are ready for the "may." All right. There may be a hell. I'm ready; where do you get off at? I have you beat any way you can look at it.

Suppose there is no hell? Suppose that when we die that ends it? I don't believe it does. I believe there is a hell and I believe there is a heaven, and just the kind of a heaven and hell that book says. But suppose that is no hell? Suppose death is eternal sleep? I believe the Bible; I believe its teachings; I have the best of you in this life. I will live longer, be happier, and have lost nothing by believing and obeying the Bible, even if there is no hell. But suppose there is a hell? Then I'm saved and you are the fool. I have you beat again.

"What shall the end be of them that obey not the gospel of God." What will some do? Some will be stoical, some will whimper, some will turn for human sympathy. Let God answer the question. You would quarrel with me. "A lake of fire" and "a furnace of fire." "In hell he lifted up his eyes, being in torment." "Eternal damnation." "The smoke of their torment ascendeth forever and ever." Let God answer the question. "What shall be the end of them that obey not the gospel of God?" Will you say, "God, I didn't have time enough?" "Behold! Now is the accepted time." Will you say, "God, I had no light?" But "light is come into the world, and men love darkness rather than light."

I stand on the shores of eternity and cry out, "Eternity! Eternity! How long, how long art thou?" Back comes the answer, "How long?"

"How long sometimes a day appears and weeks, how long are they?
They move as if the months and years would never pass away;
But months and years are passing by, and soon must all be gone,
Day by day, as the moments fly, eternity comes on.
All these must have an end; eternity has none,
It will always have as long to run as when it first begun."

"What shall be the end of them that obey not the Gospel of God?"

When Voltaire, the famous infidel, lay dying, he summoned the physician and said, "Doctor, I will give you all I have to save my life six months."

The doctor said, "You can't live six hours."

Then said Voltaire, "I'll go to hell and you'll go with me."

Hobbes, the famous English infidel, said: "I am taking a leap into the night."

When King Charles IX, who gave the order for the massacre of St. Bartholomew's day, when blood ran like water and 130,000 fell dead, when King Charles lay dying, he cried out, "O God, how will it end? Blood, blood, rivers of blood. I am lost!" And with a shriek he leaped into the hell.

King Philip of Spain said; "I wish to God I had never lived," and then in a sober thought he said: "Yes, I wish I had, but that I had lived in the fear and love of God."

Wesley said, "I shall be satisfied when I awake in His likeness."

Florence A. Foster said, "Mother, the hilltops are covered with angels; they beckon me homeward; I bid you good-bye."

Frances E. Willard cried, "How beautiful to die and be with God."

Moody cried: "Earth recedes, heaven opens, God is calling me. This is to be my coronation day."

Going to the World's Fair in Chicago, a special train on the Grand Trunk, going forty miles an hour, dashed around a curve at Battle Creek, and headed in on a sidetrack where a freight train stood. The rear brakeman had forgotten to close the switch and the train rounded the curve, dashed into the open switch and struck the freight train loaded with iron, and there was an awful wreck. The cars telescoped and the flames rushed out. Pinioned in the wreck, with steel girders bent around her, was a woman who lived in New York. Her name was Mrs. Van Dusen. She removed her diamond ear-rings, took her gold watch and chain from about her neck, slipped her rings from her fingers and handing out her purse gave her husband's address, and then said: "Gentlemen, stand back! I am a Christian and I will die like a Christian."

They leaped to their task. They tore like demons to liberate her and she started to sing,

> "My heavenly home is bright and fair.
> I'm going to die no more."

Strong men, who had looked into the cannon's mouth, fainted. She cried out, above the roar of the wind and the shrieks of the dying men, "Oh, men, don't imperil your lives for me. I am a Christian and I will die like a Christian! Stand back, men," and then she began to sing," Nearer, My God, to Thee."

"There is a way that seemeth right unto man, but the end thereof are the ways of death." Moses may have made some mistakes, but I want to tell you Moses never made a mistake when he wrote these words: "Their rock is not as our Rock, even our enemies themselves being the judges" He never made a mistake when he wrote these words. I say to you, you are going to live on and on until the constellations of the heavens are snuffed out. You are going to live on and on until the rocks crumble into dust through age. You are going to live on and on and on, until the mountain peaks are incinerated and blown by the breath of God to the four corners of infinity. "What shall the end be?" Listen! Listen!

I used to live in Pennsylvania, and of the many wonderful things for which this wonderful state has been noted, not the least is the fact that most always she has had godly men for governors, and one of the most magnificent examples of godly piety that ever honored this state was Governor Pollock. When he was governor, a young man, in a drunken brawl, shot a companion. He was tried and sentenced to be executed. They circulated a petition, brought it to Harrisburg to the governor, and the committee that waited upon the governor, among them some of his own friends, pleaded with him to commute the sentence to life imprisonment. Governor Pollock listened to their pleadings and said, "Gentlemen, I can't do it. The law must take its course." Then the ministers—Catholic and Protestant—brought a petition, and among the committee was the governor's own pastor. He approached him in earnestness, put a hand on either shoulder, begged, prayed to God to give him wisdom to grant the request. Governor Pollock listened to their petition, tears streamed down his cheeks and he said, "Gentlemen, I can't do it. I can't; I can't."

At last the boy's mother came. Her eyes were red, her cheeks sunken, her lips ashen, her hair disheveled, her clothing unkempt, her body tottering from the loss of food and sleep. Broken-hearted, she reeled, staggered and dragged herself into the presence of the governor. She pleaded for her boy. She said, "Oh, governor, let me die. Oh, governor, let him go; let me behind the bars. Oh, governor, I beg of you to let my boy go; don't, don't hang him!" And Governor Pollock listened. She staggered to his side, put her arms around him. He took her arms from his shoulder, held her at arms' length, looked into her face and said to her: "Mother, mother, I can't do it, I can't," and he ran from her presence. She screamed and fell to the floor and they carried her out.

Governor Pollock said to his secretary. "John, if I can't pardon him I can tell him how to die." He went to the cell, opened God's Word, prayed, talked of Jesus. Heaven bent near, the angels waited, and then on lightning wing sped back to glory with the glad tidings that a soul was born again. And the governor left, wishing him well for the ordeal. Shortly after he had gone, the prisoner said to the watchman, "Who was that man that talked and prayed with me?" He said, "Great God, man, don't you know? That was Governor Pollock." He threw his hands to his head and cried: "My God! My God! The governor here and I didn't know it? Why didn't you tell me that was the governor and I would have thrown my arms about him, buried my fingers in his flesh and would have said, 'Governor, I'll not let you go unless you pardon me; I'll not let you go.'" A few days later, when he stood at the scaffold, feet strapped, hands tied, noose about his necks, black cap and shroud on, just before the trap was sprung he cried, "My God! The governor there and I—" He shot down.

You can't stand before God in the Judgment and say, "Jesus, were you down there in the tabernacle? In my home? In my lodge? Did you want to save me?" Behold! Behold! A being greater than the governor is here. Jesus Christ, the Son of God, and he waits to be gracious.

"What shall the end be of them that obey not the gospel of God?"

Heaven

What do I want most of all? A man in Chicago said to me one day, "If I could have all I wanted of any one thing I would take money." He would be a fool, and so would you if you would make a similar choice. There's lots of things money can't do. Money can't buy life; money can't buy health. Andrew Carnegie says, "Anyone who can assure men ten years of life can name his price."

If you should meet with an accident which would require a surgical operation or your life would be despaired of, there is not a man here but would gladly part with all the money he has if that would give him the assurance that he could live twelve months longer.

If you had all the money in the world you couldn't go to the graveyard and put those loved ones back in your arms and have them sit once more in the family circle and hear their voices and listen to their prattle.

A steamer tied up at her wharf, had just returned from an expedition, and as the people walked down the plank their friends met them to congratulate them on their success or encourage them through their defeat. Down came a man I used to know in Fargo, S. D. Friends rushed up and said, "Why, we hear that you were very fortunate."

"Yes, wife and I left here six months ago with hardly anything. Now we have $350,000 in gold dust in the hold of the ship."

Then somebody looked around and said, "Mr. L, where is your little boy?"

The tears rolled down his cheeks and he said, "We left him buried on the banks of the Yukon beneath the snow and ice, and we would gladly part with all the gold, if we only had our boy."

But all the wealth of the Klondike could not open the grave and put that child back in their arms. Money can't buy the peace of God that passeth understanding. Money can't take the sin out of your life.

Is there any particular kind of life you would like? If you could live one hundred years you wouldn't want to die, would you? I wouldn't. I think there is always something the matter with a fellow that wants to die. I want to stay as long as God will let me stay, but when God's time comes for me to go I'm ready, any hour of the day or night. God can waken me at midnight or in the morning and I'm ready to respond. But if I could live a million years I'd like to stay. I don't want to die. I'm having a good time. God made this world for us to have a good time in. It's nothing but sin that has damned the world and brought it to misery and corruption. God wants you to have a good time. Well, then, how can I get this life that you want and everybody wants, eternal life?

If you are ill the most natural thing for you to do is to go for your doctor. You say, "I don't want to die. Can you help me?"

He looks at you and says, "I have a hundred patients on my hands, all asking the same thing. Not one of them wants to die. They ask me to use my skill and bring to bear all I have learned, but I can't fight back death. I can prescribe for your malady, but I can't prevent death."

Well, go to your philosopher. He it is that reasons out the problems and mysteries of life by the application of reason. Say to him, "Good philosopher, I have come to you for help. I want to live forever and you say that you have the touch-stone of philosophy and that you can describe and solve. Can you help me?"

He says to you, "Young man, my hair and my beard have grown longer and as white as snow, my eyes are dim, my brows are wrinkled, my form bent with the weight of years, my bones are brittle and I am just as far from the solution of that mystery and problem as when I started. I, too, sir, must soon die and sleep beneath the sod."

In my imagination I have stood by the bedside of the dying Pullman-palace-car magnate, George M. Pullman, whose will was probated at $25,000,000, and I have said, "Oh, Mr. Pullman, you will not die, you can bribe death." And I see the pupils of his eyes dilate, his breast heaves, he gasps—and is no more. The undertaker comes and makes an incision in his left arm, pumps in the embalming fluid, beneath whose mysterious power he turns as rigid as ice, and as white as alabaster, and they put his embalmed body in the rosewood coffin, trimmed with silver and gold, and then they put that in a hermetically sealed casket.

The grave-diggers go to Graceland Cemetery, on the shore of Lake Michigan, and dig his grave in the old family lot, nine feet wide, and they put in there Portland cement four and a half feet thick, while it is yet soft, pliable and plastic. A set of workmen drop down into the grave a steel cage with steel bars one inch apart. They bring his body, in the hermetically sealed casket all wrapped about with cloth, and they lower it into the steel cage, and a set of workmen put steel bars across the top and another put concrete and a solid wall of masonry and they bring it up within eighteen inches of the surface; they put back the black loamy soil, then they roll back the sod and with a whisk broom and dust pan they sweep up the dirt, and you would never know that there sleeps the Pullman-palace-car magnate, waiting for the trumpet of Gabriel to sound; for the powers of God will snap his steel, cemented sarcophagus as though it were made of a shell and he will stand before God as any other man.

What does your money amount to? What does your wealth amount to?

I summon the three electrical wizards of the world to my bedside and I say, "Gentlemen I want to live and I have sent for you to come," and they say to me, "Mr. Sunday, we will flash messages across the sea without wires; we can illuminate the homes and streets of your city and drive your trolley cars and we can kill men with electricity, but we can't prolong life."

And I summon the great Queen Elizabeth, queen of an empire upon which the sun never sets. Three thousand dresses hung in her wardrobe. Her jewels were measured by the peck. Dukes, kings, earls fought for her smiles. I stand by her bedside and I hear her cry "All my possessions for one moment of time!"

I go to Alexander the Great, who won his first battle when he was eighteen, and was King of Macedonia when he was twenty. He sat down on the shore of the Ægean sea, wrapped the drapery of his couch about him and lay down to eternal sleep, the conqueror of all the known world, when he was thirty-five years of age.

I go to Napoleon Bonaparte. Victor Hugo called him the archangel of war. He arose in the air of the nineteenth century like a meteor. His sun rose at Austerlitz; it set at Waterloo. He leaped over the slain of his countrymen to be first consul; and then he vaulted to the throne of the emperor of France. But it was the cruel wanton achievement of insatiate and unsanctified ambition and it led to the barren St. Helena isle. As the storm beat upon the rock, once more he fought at the head of his troops at Austerlitz, at Mt. Tabor, and the Pyramids. Once more he cried, "I'm still the head of the army," and he fell back, and the greatest warrior the world has known since the days of Joshua, was no more. Tonight on the banks of the Seine he lies in his magnificent tomb, with his marshals sleeping where he can summon them, and the battle flags he made famous draped around him, and from the four corners of the earth students and travelers turn aside to do homage to the great military genius.

I want to show you the absolute and utter futility of pinning your hope to a lot of fool things that will damn your soul to hell. There is only one way: "As Moses lifted up the serpent in the wilderness, even so must the Son of Man be lifted up, that whosoever believeth in him should not perish, but have eternal life. For God so loved the world that he gave his only begotten Son, that whosoever believeth in him should not perish, but have everlasting life." Search the annals of time and the pages of history and where do you find promises like that? Only upon the pages of the Bible do you find them.

You want to live and so do I. You want eternal life and so do I, and I want you to have it. The next question I want to ask is, how can you get it? You have seen things that won't give it to you. How can you get it? All you have tonight or ever will have you will come into possession of in one of three ways—honestly, dishonestly, or as a gift. Honestly: You will work and sweat and therefore give an honest equivalent for what you get. Dishonestly: You will steal. Third, as a gift, you will inherit it. And eternal life must come to you in one of these three ways.

A great many people believe in a high moral standard. They deal honestly in business and are charitable, but if you think that is going to save you, you are the most mistaken man on God's earth, and you will be the biggest disappointed being that ever lived. You can't hire a substitute in religion. You can't do some deed of kindness or act of philanthropy and substitute that for the necessity of repentance and faith in

Jesus Christ. Lots of people will acknowledge their sin in the world, struggle on without Jesus Christ, and do their best to live honorable, upright lives. Your morality will make you a better man or woman, but it will never save your soul in the world.

Supposing you had an apple tree that produced sour apples and you wanted to change the nature of it, and you would ask the advice of people. One would say prune it, and you would buy a pruning hook and cut off the superfluous limbs. You gather the apples and they are still sour. Another man says to fertilize it, and you fertilize it and still it doesn't change the nature of it. Another man says spray it to kill the caterpillars, but the apples are sour just the same. Another man says introduce a graft of another variety.

When I was a little boy, one day my grandfather said to me: "Willie, come on," and he took a ladder and beeswax, a big jackknife, a saw and some cloth, and we went into the valley. He leaned the ladder against a sour crab-apple tree, climbed up and sawed off some of the limbs, split them and shoved in them some pear sprouts as big as my finger and twice as long, and around them he tied a string and put in some beeswax. I said, "Grandpa, what are you doing?" He said, "I'm grafting pear sprouts into the sour crab." I said, "What will grow, crab apples or pears?" He said, "Pears; I don't know that I'll ever live to eat the pear—I hope I may—but I know you will." I lived to see those sprouts which were no longer than my finger grow as large as any limb and I climbed the tree and picked and ate the pears. He introduced a graft of another variety and that changed the nature of the tree.

And so you can't change yourself with books. That which is flesh is flesh, no matter whether it is cultivated flesh, or ignorant flesh or common, ordinary flesh. That which is flesh is flesh, and all your lodges, all your money on God Almighty's earth can never change your nature. Never. That's got to come by and through repentance and faith in Jesus Christ. That's the only way you will ever get it changed. We have more people with fool ways trying to get into heaven, and there's only one way to do and that is by and through repentance and faith in Jesus Christ.

Here are two men. One man born with hereditary tendencies toward bad, a bad father, a bad mother and bad grandparents. He has bad blood in his veins and he turns as naturally to sin as a duck to water. There he is, down and out, a booze fighter and the off-scouring scum of the earth. I go to him in his squalor and want and unhappiness, and say to him: "God has included all that sin that he may have mercy on all. All have sinned and come short of the glory of God. Will you accept Jesus Christ as your Saviour?"

"Whosoever cometh unto me I will in no wise cast out," and that man says to me, "No, I don't want your Christ as my Saviour."

Here is a man with hereditary tendencies toward good, a good father, a good mother, good grandparents, lived in a good neighborhood, was taught to go to Sunday School and has grown up to be a good, earnest, upright, virtuous, responsible business man; his name is synonymous with all that is pure and kind, and true. His name is as good as a government bond at any bank for a reasonable amount. Everybody respects him. He is generous, charitable and kind. I go to your high-toned, cultured, respectable man and say to him: "God hath included all under sin that he might have mercy upon all. All have sinned and come short of the glory of God. Whosoever cometh unto me I will in no wise cast out. Will you accept Jesus Christ as your Saviour? Will you give me your hand?" He says: "No, sir; I don't want your Christ."

What's the difference between those two men? Absolutely none. They are both lost. Both are going to hell. God hasn't one way of saving the one and another way of saving the other fellow. God will save that man if he accepts Christ and he will do the same for the other fellow. That man is a sinner and this man is a sinner. That man is lower in sin than this man, but they both say, "No" to Jesus Christ and they are both lost or God is a liar.

You don't like it? I don't care a rap whether you do or not. You'll take it or go to hell. Stop doing what you think will save you and do what God says will save you.

Morality doesn't save anybody. Your culture doesn't save you. I don't care who you are or how good you are, if you reject Jesus Christ you are doomed. God hasn't one plan of salvation for the millionaire and another for the hobo. He has the same plan for everybody. God isn't going to ask you whether you like it or not, either. He isn't going to ask you your opinion of his plan. There it is and we'll have to take it as God gives it.

You come across a lot of fools who say there are hypocrites in the Church. What difference does that make? Are you the first person that has found that out and are you fool enough to go to hell because they are going to hell? If you are, don't come to me and expect me to think you have any sense. Not all all. Not for a minute.

A good many people attend church because it adds a little bit to their respectability. That is proof positive to me that the Gospel is a good thing. This is a day when good things are counterfeited. You never saw anybody counterfeiting brown paper. No, it isn't worth it. You have seen them counterfeiting Christians? Yes. You have seen counterfeit money? Yes. You never saw a counterfeit infidel. They counterfeit religion. Certainly. A hypocrite is a counterfeit.

But there is one class of these people that I haven't very much respect for. They are so good, so very good, that they are absolutely good for nothing. A woman came to me and said: "Mr. Sunday, I haven't sinned in ten years."

I said: "You lie, I think."

Well, a man says: "Look here, there must be something in morality, because so many people trust in it." Would vice become virtue because more people follow it? Simply because more people follow it doesn't make a wrong right; not at all.

There was an old Spaniard, Ponce de Leon, who searched through the glades of Florida. He thought away out there in the midst of the tropical vegetation was a fountain of perpetual youth, which, if he could only find and dip beneath its water would smooth the wrinkles from his brow and make his gray hair turn like the raven's wing. Did he ever find it? No, it never existed. It was all imagination. And there are people today searching for something that doesn't exist. Salvation doesn't exist in morality, in reformation, in paying your debts. It doesn't exist in being true to your marriage vows. It is only by repentance and faith in the atoning blood of Jesus Christ, and some of you fellows have searched for it until you are gray-haired, and you will never find it because it only exists in one place—repentance and faith in Jesus Christ.

Supposing I had in one hand a number of kernels of wheat and a number of diamonds equal in number and size to the kernels of wheat. I would say: "Take your choice." Nine of ten would take the diamonds. I would say: "Diamonds are worth more than wheat." So they are now, but you take those diamonds, they will never grow, never add. But I can take a handful of wheat, sow it, and, fecundated by the rays of the sun and the moisture, it will grow and in a few years I have what's worth all the diamonds in the world, for wheat contains the power of life; wheat can reproduce and diamonds can't; they're not life. A diamond is simply a piece of charcoal changed by the mysterious process of nature, but it has no life. Wheat has life. Wheat can grow. You can take a moral man; he may shine and glisten and sparkle like a diamond. He may outshine in his beauty the Christian man. But he will never be anything else. His morality can never grow. It has no life, but the man who is a Christian has life. He has eternal life. Your morality is a fine thing until death comes, then it's lost and you are lost. Your diamond is a fine thing to carry until it's lost, and of what value is it then? Of what value is your morality when your soul is lost?

Supposing I go out in the spring and I see two farmers, living across the road from each other. One man plows his field and then harrows and puts on the roller, gets it all fine and then plants the corn or drills in the oats. I come back in the fall and that man has gathered his crop into the barn and the granaries and has hay stacked around the barn.

The other fellow is plowing and puts the roller on and gets his ground in good shape. I come back in the fall and he is still doing the same thing. I say, "What are you doing?" He says: "Well, I believe in a high state of cultivation." I say: "Look at your neighbor, see what he has." "A barn full of grain." "Yes." "More stock." "Yes." But he says: "Look at the weeds. You don't see any weeds like that on my place. Why, he had to burn the weeds before he could find the potatoes to dig them. The weeds were as big as the corn." I said: "I'll agree with you that he has raised some weeds, but he has raised corn as well." What is that ground worth without seed in it? No more than your life is worth without having Jesus Christ in it. You will starve to death if you don't put seed in the ground. Plowing the ground without putting in the seed doesn't amount to a snap of the finger.

When I was a little boy out in Iowa, at the end of the term of school it was customary for the teachers to give us little cards, with a hand in one corner holding a scroll and in that scroll was a place to write the name: "Willie Sunday, good boy." Willie Sunday never got hump-shouldered lugging them home, I can tell you. I never carried off the champion long-distance belt for verse-quoting, either. If you ever saw an American kid, I was one.

I feel sorry for the little Lord Fauntleroy boys with long curly hair and white stockings. Yank 'em off and let them go barefoot.

A friend of mine told me he was one time being driven along the banks of the Hudson and they went past a beautiful farm, and there sitting on the fence in front of a tree, in which was fastened a mirror about twelve inches square, sat a bird of paradise that was looking into the mirror, adjusting his plumage and admiring himself, and the farmer who had driven my friends out said that every time he passed those birds were doing that.

I thought, "Well, that reminds me of a whole lot of fools I'm fortunate enough to meet everywhere. They sit before the mirror of culture, and their mirror of money, and their mirror of superior education and attainments; they are married into some old families. What does God care about that?" I suppose some of you spent a whole lot of money to plant a family tree, but I warrant you keep to the back the limbs on which some of your ancestors were hanged for stealing horses.

You are mistaken in God's plan of salvation. Some people seem to think God is like a great big bookkeeper in heaven and that he has a whole lot of angels as assistants. Every time you do a good thing he writes it down on one page and every time you do a bad deed he writes it down on the opposite page, and when you die he draws a line and adds them up. If you have done more good things than bad, you go to heaven; more bad things than good, go to hell. You would be dumfounded how many people have sense about other things that haven't any sense about religion. As though that was God's plan of redemption. Your admission into heaven depends upon your acceptance of Jesus Christ; reject him and God says you will be damned.

Back in the time of Noah, I have no doubt there were a lot of good folks. There was Noah. God says: "Look here, Noah, I'm going to drown this world with a flood and I want you to go to work and make an ark." And Noah started to make it according to God's instructions and he pounded, and sawed, and drove nails and worked for 120 years, and I have often imagined the comments of the gang in an automobile going by. They say: "Look at the old fool Noah building an ark. Does he ever expect God's going to get water enough to flood that?" Along comes another crowd and one says: "That Noah bunch is getting daffy on religion. I think we'd better take them before the commission and pass upon their sanity." Along comes another crowd and they say: "Well, there's that Noah crowd. I guess we won't invite them to our card party after Lent is over." They said: "Why, they're too religious. We'll just let them alone."

Noah paid no heed to their criticism, but went on working until he got through. God gave the crowd a chance, but they didn't heed. It started to rain and it rained and rained until the rivers and creeks leaped their banks and the lowlands were flooded. Then the people began to move to the hilltops. The water began to creep up the hills. Then I can see the people hurrying off to lumber yards to buy lumber to build little rafts of their own, for they began to see that Noah wasn't such a fool after all. The hilltops became inundated and it crept to the mountains and the mountains became submerged. Until the flood came that crowd was just as well off as Noah, but when the flood struck them Noah was saved and they were lost, because Noah trusted God and they trusted in themselves. You moral men, you may be just as well off as the Christian until death knocks you down, then you are lost, because you trust in your morality. The Christian is saved because he trusts in Jesus. Do you see where you lose out?

"Without the shedding of blood there is no remission of sin." You must accept the atonement Christ made by shedding his blood or God will slam the gate of heaven in your face.

Some people, you know, want to wash their sins and they whitewash them, but God wants them white, and there's a lot of difference between being "white-washed" and "washed white."

Supposing I was at one of your banks this morning and they gave me $25 in gold. Supposing I would put fifty of your reputable citizens on this platform and they would all substantiate what I say, and supposing I would be authorized by the bank to say that they would give every man and woman that stands in line in front of the bank at 9 o'clock in the morning, $25 in gold. If I could stand up there and make that announcement in this city with confidence in my word, people would line the streets and string away back on the hills, waiting for the bank to open.

I can stand here and tell you that God offers you salvation through repentance and faith in Jesus Christ and that you must accept it or be lost, and you will stand up and argue the question, as though your argument can change God's plan. You never can do it. Not only has God promised you salvation on the grounds of your acceptance of Jesus Christ as your Saviour, but he has promised to give you a home in which to spend eternity. Listen! "In my Father's house are many mansions; if it were not so I would have told you. I go to prepare a place for you." Some people say heaven is a state or condition. I don't believe it. It might possibly be better to be in a heavenly state than in a heavenly place. It might be better to be in hell in a heavenly state than to be in heaven in a hellish state. That may be true. Heaven is as much a place as the home to which you are going when I dismiss the meeting is a place. "I go to prepare a place for you." Heaven is a place where there are going to be some fine folks. Abraham will be there and I'm going up to see him. Noah, Moses, Joseph, Jacob, Isaiah, Daniel, Jeremiah the weeping prophet, Paul, John, Peter, James, Samuel, Martin Luther, Spurgeon, Calvin, Moody. Oh, heaven is a place where there will be grand and noble people, and all who believe in Jesus will be there.

Suppose instead of turning off the gas at bedtime I blew it out. Then when Nell and I awoke choking, instead of opening the window and turning off the gas I got a bottle of cologne and sprinkled ourselves. The fool principle of trying to overcome the poison of gas with perfumery wouldn't work. The next day there would be a coroner's jury in the house. Your principle of trying to overcome sin by morality won't work either.

I'm going to meet David and I'll say: "David, I'm not a U.P., but I wish you'd sing the twenty-third psalm for me."

The booze fighter won't be in heaven; he is here. The skeptic won't be there; he is here. There'll be nobody to run booze joints or gambling hells in heaven. Heaven will be a place of grand and noble people, who love Jesus. The beloved wife will meet her husband. Mother, you will meet your babe again that you have been separated from for months or years. Heaven will be free from everything that curses and damns this old world here. Wouldn't this be a grand old world if it weren't for a lot of things in it? Can you conceive anything being grander than this world if it hadn't a lot of things in it? The only thing that makes it a decent place to live in is the religion of Jesus Christ. There isn't a man that would live in it if you took religion out. Your mills would rot on their foundations if there were no Christian people of influence here.

There will be no sickness in heaven, no pain, no sin, no poverty, no want, no death, no grinding toil. "There remaineth therefore a rest to the people of God." I tell you there are a good many poor men and women that never have any rest. They have had to get up early in the morning and work all day, but in heaven there remaineth a rest for the people of God. Weary women that start out early to their daily toil, you won't have to get out and toil all day. No toil in heaven, no sickness. "God shall wipe away all tears from their eyes." You will not be standing watching with a heart filled with expectation, and doubt, and hope. No watching the undertaker screw the coffin lid over your loved one, or watching the pall-bearers carrying out the coffin and hearing the preacher say, "Ashes to ashes, dust to dust." None of that in heaven. Heaven—that is a place He has gone to prepare for those who will do his will and keep his commandments and turn from their sin. Isn't it great?

Everything will be perfect in heaven. Down here we only know in part, but there we will know as we are known. It is a city that hath foundation. Here we have no continuing state. Look at your beautiful homes. You admire them. The next time you go up your avenues and streets look at the homes. But they are going to rot on their foundations. Every one of them. Where are you tonight, old Eternal City of Rome on your seven hills? Where are you? Only a memory of your glory. Where have they all gone? The homes will crumble.

"Enoch walked with God and was not, for God took him." That is a complete biography of Enoch.

Elijah was carried to heaven in a chariot of fire and Elisha took up the mantle of the prophet Elijah and smote the Jordan and went back to the seminary where Elijah had taught and told the people there. They would not believe him, and they looked for Elijah, but they found him not. Centuries later it was the privilege of Peter, James, and John in the company of Jesus Christ, on the Mount of Transfiguration, to look into the face of that same Elijah who centuries before had walked the hilltops and slain four hundred and fifty of the prophets of Baal.

Stephen, as they stoned him to death, with his face lighted up saw

Jesus standing on the right of God the Father, the place which he had designated before his crucifixion would be his abiding place until the fulfilment of the time of the Gentiles in the world. Among the last declarations of Jesus is, "In my Father's house are many mansions." What a comfort to the bereaved and afflicted. Not only had God provided salvation through faith in Jesus Christ as a gift from God's outstretched hand, but he provided a home in which you can spend eternity. He has provided a home for you. Surely, surely, friends, from the beginning of the history of man, from the time Enoch walked with God and was not, until John on the island of Patmos saw the new Jerusalem let down by God out of heaven, we have ample proof that heaven is a place. Although we cannot see it with the natural eyes, it is a place, the dwelling place of God and of the angels and of the redeemed through faith in the Son of God.

He says, "I go to prepare a place for you."

People some times ask me, "Who do you think will die first, Mr. Sunday, you or your wife, or your children or your mother?" I don't know. I think I will. I never expect to be an old man, I work too hard. I burn up more energy preaching in an hour any other man will burn up in ten or twelve hours. I never expect to live to be an old man. I don't expect to, but I know this much, if my wife or my babies should go first this old world would be a dark place for me and I would be glad when God summoned me to leave it; and if I left first I know they would be glad when God called them home. If I go first, I know after I go up and take Jesus by the hand and say, "Jesus, thank you. I'm glad you honored me with the privilege of preaching your Gospel; I wish I could have done it better, but I did my best, and now, Jesus, if you don't care, I'd like to hang around the gate and be the first to welcome my wife and the babies when they come. Do you care, Jesus, if I sit there?" And he will say, "No, you can sit right there, Bill, if you want to; it's all right." I'll say, "Thank you, Lord."

If they would go first, I think after they would go up and thank Jesus that they are home, they would say, "Jesus, I wish you would hurry up and bring papa home. He doesn't want to stay down there because we are up here." They would go around and put their grips away in their room, wherever it is, and then they would say, "Can we sit here, Jesus?" "Yes, that's all right."

I don't know where I'll live when I get to heaven. I don't know whether I'll live on a main street or an avenue or a boulevard. I don't know where I'll live when I get to heaven. I don't know whether it will be in the back alley or where, but I'll just be glad to get there. I'll be thankful for the mansion wherever God provides it. I never like to think about heaven as a great, big tenement house, where they put hundreds of people under one roof, as we do in Chicago or other big cities. "In my Father's house are many mansions." And so it will be up in heaven, and I'll be glad, awfully glad, and I tell you I think if my wife and children go first, the children might be off some place playing, but wife would be right there, and I would meet her and say, "Why, wife, where are the children?" She would say, "Why, they are playing on the banks of the river." (We are told about the river that flows from the throne of God.) We would walk down and I would say, "Hello, Helen! Hey, George. Hey, Willsky; bring the baby; come on." And they would come tearing as they do now,

I would say, "Now, children, run away and play a little while. I haven't seen mother for a long time and we have lot of things to talk about," and I think we would walk away and sit down under a tree and I would put my head in her lap as I do now when my head is tired, and I would say, "Wife, a whole lot of folks down there in our neighborhood in Chicago have died; have they come to heaven?"

"Well, I don't know. Who has died?"

"Mr. S. Is he here?"

"I haven't seen him."

"No? His will probated five million. Bradstreet and Dun rated him AaG. Isn't he here?"

"I haven't seen him."

"Is Mr. J. here?"

"I haven't seen him."

"Haven't seen him, wife? That's funny. He left years before I did. Is Mrs. N. here?"

"No."

"You know they lived on River street. Her husband paid $8,000 for a lot and $60,000 for a house. He paid $2,000 for a bathroom. Mosaic floor and the finest of fixtures. You know, wife, she always came to church late and would drive up in her carriage, and she would sweep down the aisle and you would think all the perfume of Arabia had floated in, and she had diamonds in her ears as big as pebbles. Is she here?"

"I haven't seen her."

"Well! Well! Well! Is Aunty Griffith here?"

"Yes; aunty lives next to us."

"I knew she would be here. God bless her heart! She had two big lazy, drunken louts of boys that didn't care for her, and the church supported her for sixteen years to my knowledge and they put her in the home for old people. Hello, yonder she comes. How are you, Aunty?"

She will say, "How are you, William?"

"I'm first rate."

"Mon, ye look natural just the same."

"Yes."

"And when did ye leave Chicago, Wally?"

"Last night, Aunty."

"I'm awfully glad to see you, and, Wally, I live right next door to you, mon."

"Good, Aunty, I knew God would let you in. My, where's mother, wife?"

"She's here."

"I know she's here; I wish she would come. Helen, is that mother coming down the hill?"

"Yes."

I would say, "Have you see Fred, or Rody, or Peacock, or Ackley, or any of them?"

"Yes. They live right around near us."

"George, you run down and tell Fred I've come, will you? Hunt up Rody, and Peacock and Ackley and Fred, and see if you can find Frances around there and tell them I've just come in." And they would come and I would say, "How are you? Glad to see you. Feeling first-rate."

And, oh, what a time we'll have in heaven. In heaven they never mar the hillsides with spades, for they dig no graves. In heaven they never telephone for the doctor, for nobody gets sick. In heaven no one carries handkerchiefs, for nobody cries. In heaven they never telephone for the undertaker, for nobody dies. In heaven you will never see a funeral procession going down the street, nor crêpe hanging from the doorknob. In heaven, none of the things that enter your home here will enter there. Sickness won't get in; death won't get in, nor sorrow, because "Former things are passed away," all things have become new. In heaven the flowers never fade, the winter winds and blasts never blow. The rivers never congeal, never freeze, for it never gets cold. No, sir.

Say, don't let God be compelled to hang a "For Rent" sign in the window of the mansion he has prepared for you. I would walk around with him and I'd say, "Whose mansion is that, Jesus?"

"Why, I had that for one of the rich men, but he passed it up."

"Who's that one for?"

"That was for a doctor, but he did not take it."

"That was for one of the school teachers, but she didn't come."

"Who is that one for, Jesus?"

"That was for a society man, but he didn't want it."

"Who is that one for?"

"That was for a booze fighter, but he wouldn't pass up the business."

Don't let God hang a "For Rent" sign in the mansion that he has prepared for you. Just send up word and say, "Jesus, I've changed my mind; just put my name down for that, will you? I'm coming. I'm coming." "In my Father's house are many mansions; if it were not so I would have told you; I go to prepare a place for you."

Appendix

Sundayisms

The Bible will always be full of things you cannot understand, as long as you will not live according to those you can understand.

Some of the biggest lies ever told are to be found on gravestones.

There are men in hell because they wasted too much time in trying to find out where Cain got his wife.

I would rather have standing room in heaven than own the world and go to hell.

I am against anything that the devil is in favor of.

Hell is the highest reward that the devil can offer you for being a servant of his.

I drive the same kind of nails all orthodox preachers do. The only difference is that they use a tack hammer and I use a sledge.

Some preachers need the cushions of their chairs upholstered oftener than they need their shoes half-soled.

You can preach sociology, or psychology, or any other kind of ology, but if you leave Jesus Christ out of it you hit the tobboggan slide to hell.

We've got a bunch of preachers breaking their necks to please a lot of old society dames.

There are a good many things worse than living and dying an old maid, and one of them is marrying the wrong man.

A saloon-keeper and a good mother don't pull on the same rope.

You can't raise the standard of women's morals by raising their pay envelopes. It lies deeper than that.

When you quit living like the devil I will quit preaching that way.

If you took no more care of yourself physically than spiritually, you'd be just as dried up physically as you are spiritually.

It takes a big man to see other people succeed without raising a howl.

Pilate washed his hands. If he had washed his old black heart he would have been all right.

Your reputation is what people say about you. Your character is what God and your wife know about you.

I have no faith in a woman who talks about heaven and makes hell out of her home.

The best time for a man to sow his wild oats is between the ages of eighty-five and ninety.

Sin flourishes because folks treat it like a cream puff.

They tell me a revival is only temporary; so is a bath, but it does you good.

When Church members stop voting for the saloon, liquor will go to hell.

People do not go to church because it's their duty. The majority go because they want to.

I contend there should be some visible connection between the thing a man believes in and himself.

I once heard of a blind man who carried a lighted lantern to keep people from stumbling over him. Hold up your light so others won't stumble over you.

Most of the useful work of the world is done by ordinary people.

We spend too much time twisting garlands for the "remarkable" people, building thrones for the great, sculpturing warriors, and forgetting "ordinary" people.

Exceptional things are not to be depended upon. Better trust the smallest planet than a dozen comets for steady light.

A lamp is better than a rocket.

The world is wrong side up. It needs to be turned upside down in order to be right side up.

Some speak of religion as though it were refined imbecility or a shower of spiritual cocaine.

The old world is horribly disordered and out of joint; it must come under Omnipotent surgery before we can expect health.

When religion comes in the front door, mirth and laughter will not go out the back door.

A preacher complaining about my language asked me: "Why don't you preach like I do?" I told him if I did, I wouldn't be any better than he was.

God didn't make two sets of moral laws. What's wrong for the goose is wrong for the gander.

A lot of churches don't need an evangelist as much as they need an undertaker.

The average church has so much machinery and so little oil of the Holy Spirit that it squeaks like a threshing machine when you start it up in the fall after it has been out in the field all the year.

Some preachers have to be wet nurses to a lot of 200-pound babies sitting in the pews.

Don't take away from teachers the right to punish kids. I wore four pairs of pants when I went to school.

Some preachers don't believe in revivals; neither does the devil.

I'm trying to make America so dry that a man must be primed before he can spit.

Some men are miserable because they have just enough religion to give them goose pimples.

I don't use much highfalutin language. I learned long ago to put the cookies and jam on the lowest shelf.

That boy is lucky whose mother brings him up with prayer and a good hickory.

When some folks pray it reminds me of a jack rabbit eating alfalfa.

You say you have a bad temper, but it's over in a minute; so is a shotgun, but it blows everything to pieces.

When the Bible says one thing and scholarship says another, scholarship can go plumb to the devil.

The devil finds no fault with the mother who makes her children play in the street so they won't wear out the carpet.

The woman who does nothing but spin society yarns is making a rope to hang her boy.

The auto is not responsible for the falling off in church attendance. That fool thing will stand in the middle of the road until you tell it where to go. It's the man behind the wheel that's to blame.

Some homes need a hickory switch a good deal more than they do a piano.

You can't measure manhood with a tape line around the biceps.

If we people were able to have panes of glass over our hearts, some of us would want stained glass wouldn't we?

The Bible says forgive your debtors; the world says "sue them for their dough."

The man who can drive a hog and keep his religion will stand without hitching.

The man who votes for the saloon is pulling on the same rope with the devil whether he knows it or not.

Jesus Christ came among the common people. Abraham Lincoln said that God must have loved the common people: he made so many of them.

You can't shine for God on Sunday, and then be a London fog on Monday.

Give your face to God and he will put his shine on it.

I hate to see a man roll up to church in a limousine and then drop a quarter in the collection plate.

Going to church doesn't make a man a Christian, any more than going to a garage makes him an automobile.

No man has any business to be in a bad business.

It won't save your soul if your wife is a Christian. You have to be something more than a brother-in-law to the Church.

Morality isn't light; it is only the polish on the candlestick.

My Boyhood

I never saw my father. He walked from Ames, Iowa, to Des Moines, thirty miles, to enlist in the Civil War, and was assigned to Company E, Twenty-third Iowa Infantry, in August, 1862. I was born on my grandfather's farm one mile south of Ames, Story County, Iowa, the nineteenth of the following November.

My father was born near Chambersburg, Pennsylvania, and was of Pennsylvania Dutch parentage. He was a contractor and brick mason by trade, and built one of the first brick buildings ever erected in Cedar Rapids, Iowa.

He sleeps in an unknown grave beneath the eternal flowers and the perpetual sunshine of the Southland, waiting for the trumpet of Gabriel to sound the reveille on the Resurrection morning. Then, for the first time, I shall look into the face of him whose name I bear, and whose blood courses through my veins.

> No more the bugle calls the weary one;
> Rest, noble spirit, in your grave unknown.
> I shall see him and know him among the brave and true
> When a robe of white is given for his faded coat of blue.

His regiment forded a river which was partly frozen. He and scores of other soldiers caught severe colds that caused complications from which he and many others died. They were buried at Camp Patterson, Missouri, but all traces of the graves has been blotted out.

Father wrote to mother from the front lines and said, "When the baby is born, if it is a boy, name him William Ashley." So my name is William Ashley Sunday. I was born in a log cabin and lived there for years until my grandfather built a sawmill, run by water power, cut lumber from black-walnut logs, and built a frame house which stands today on the old farm near Ames. . . .

My grandfather was one of the men who helped locate the Iowa Agricultural College at Ames, now named Iowa State College. He had no money to give with which to start the college, and so he gave part of his land as his donation. He and two other men, pioneers of Story County, Dan McCarthy and L. Q. Hoggett, aided in staking out the ground and locating the first building of what has become one of the greatest schools of its class in the United States.

He and General Grant were second cousins. Both were born in Ohio. After General Grant became President, he wrote a letter inviting granddad to visit him in Washington, but it was a long, tiresome journey in those days, and expensive, too, and money was as scarce as mosquitoes in January.

Granddad wore a coonskin cap, rawhide boots, blue jeans, and said "done hit" instead of "did it," "come" instead of "came," and "seen" instead of "saw." He drank coffee out of his saucer and ate peas with his knife. He had no "soup-and-fish" suit to wear, so he did not go.

During the first three years of my life I was sickly and could scarcely walk. Mother used to carry me on a pillow which she made for that purpose. There were no resident physicians in those pioneer days, and itinerant doctors would drive up to our cabin and ask, "Anybody sick here?"

One day Doctor Avery, a Frenchman, called at our cabin and mother told him, "I have a little boy three years old who has been sick ever since he was born."

The old doctor said, "Let me see him." He gave me the once-over, while I yelled and screamed like a Comanche Indian. Then he said to mother, "I can cure that boy."

She asked him how much he would charge, and he replied, "Oh, if you will feed me and my old mare, that will pay the bill."

Mother said, "All right; but you will have to sleep up in the garret. We have no stairs and you'll have to climb the ladder."

He replied, "That suits me." He then went into the woods and picked leaves from various shrubs, including mulberry leaves and elderberries, dug up roots, and from them made a sirup and gave it to me. In a short time I was going like the wind and have been hitting on all eight ever since. From that day to this, elderberries and mulberries have been my favorite wild fruit, and I like sassafras tea. . . .

Our house was the stopping place for visiting strangers. Everybody was welcome.

Newspapers were scarce, although the country editor, with his Washington hand press and grip filled with type, was only a step behind the pioneer. The newspaper was our bible.

I used to help milk ten cows night and morning. We had one old cow, a Hereford, that could open the gate with her head, and when we tied the gate with a rope, she would untie the knot with her horns and lead the whole herd into the cornfield. I can hear the call to round up the night raiders, "Oh, boys, get up! The cows are in the corn." My, how I did hate that white-faced cow, and how happy I was when the butchers got her!

I kept up my station in the harvest field with men when only eleven years old. That was before the days of the McCormick self-binder, when the grain was cut with a foot-dropping reaper; and we bound the bundle with a band we made from the grain. I can make that band today as quick as you can bat your eye.

* * *

When my grandmother died, they would not tell me for two days. I sensed that something was wrong and asked, "Where is grandma?" They replied, "She is home." I said, "I'm going to see her." They said, "Willie, she wouldn't know you, and you wouldn't know her." I answered, "I would, too, know her."

I would leave her coffin only when forced to do so. The second day after the funeral my mother missed me. They called and searched everywhere; finally my dog picked up the scent and they followed my tracks through the snow to the graveyard, and there they found me lying across her grave, weeping and chilled through with the cold November winds. For weeks they feared that I would not live, but God spared my life and has led me where I am today.

The battle grew hard. The wolf of poverty howled and scratched at the cabin door. Mother decided to send Ed and myself to the Soldiers'

Orphans' Home at Glenwood, Iowa. There were three such homes located in the state—Glenwood, Cedar Falls, and Davenport. One of the saddest memories of my life is the recollection of the grief I felt when leaving the old farm to go to Ames to take the train for the trip to Glenwood. I had never been farther away from home than Nevada, the county seat, eight miles east.

When we climbed into the wagon to go to town I called out, "Goodby trees, good-by spring." I put my arms around my dog named Watch and kissed him.

The train left about one o'clock in the morning. We went to the little hotel near the depot to wait. That hotel was left standing for forty years.

The proprietor awakened us about twelve-thirty, saying, "The train is coming." I looked into mother's face. Her eyes were red and her cheeks wet from weeping, her hair disheveled. While Ed and I slept she had prayed and wept. We went to the depot, and as the train pulled in she drew us to her heart, sobbing as if her heart would break.

The conductor called, "All aboard!" and the train pulled out. We raised the window. With my arms outstretched toward mother I cried, "I don't want to go to the Orphans' Home. Take me back to the farm with you." And today something tugs at my heartstrings, saying:

> I want to go back to the orchard,
>   The orchard that used to be mine;
> Where the apples are redd'ning
>   And filling the air with their wine.
>
> I want to wake up in the morning
>   To the chirp of the birds in the eaves;
> I want the west wind through the cornfields
>   To rustle the leaves.
>
> I want to run on through the pasture,
>   And let down the dusty old bars;
> I want to find you there still waiting,
>   Your eyes blazing like the twin stars.

Oh, nights! you are weary and dreary;
*   And days! there's something you lack,*
To the old farm in the valley—
*   I want to go back.*

Shall I ever forget the home of my childhood? Yes; when the flowers forget the sun that kissed and warmed them. Yes; when the mountain peaks are incinerated into ashes. Yes; when love dies out in the human heart. Yes; when the desert sands grow cold.

My Conversion

I walked down State Street in Chicago one Sunday afternoon about forty years ago with some baseball players whose names were world renowned. We entered a saloon and drank, and then walked to the corner of State and Van Buren streets, which was then a vacant lot and where afterward Siegel & Cooper's big department store was erected.

I never pass that spot to this day that I do not stop, take off my hat, bow my head, and thank God for saving and keeping me. I was passing that corner one day at the noon hour as hundreds of people were pouring out of the stores and office buildings for lunch. I stepped to the edge of the sidewalk, removed my hat and bowed my head. A policeman came up and asked, "Pardner, are you sick? I saw you step to the edge of the sidewalk and remove your hat. If you are, I'll call the wagon."

"No, my name is Billy Sunday. I was converted on this spot nearly forty years ago and I never pass here that I do not stop and pray and thank God for saving me. I was praying—that's why I removed my hat."

The policeman removed his cap, and stretching out his hand he said, "Put her there, Bill. I know who you are; you stay and pray as long as you want to and I'll keep the gang away from you."

As we came to the corner of State and Van Buren streets, some men and women were in a Gospel wagon, playing instruments and singing Gospel hymns that I heard my mother sing in the log cabin out in Iowa. We sat on the curbstone and listened. A man arose. His name was Harry Monroe, an ex-gambler and "shover of the queer"—that is, he passed counterfeit money for a gang of counterfeiters. He became converted and was for twenty-five years superintendent of the old Pacific Garden Mission, 100 East Van Buren Street, Chicago, which was established by Colonel George Clark fifty-five years ago, and there has not been a night in all these years that someone has not accepted Christ as Saviour in that mission.

Well, we sat on the curb listening to men and women playing on cornets and trombones and singing Gospel hymns that many of the churches have blue-penciled as being too crude for these so-called enlightened days; but these hymns stir memories that drive folks back to their mother's God and Christ, and, compared with this, semi-jazz, rattle-trap, dishwater music is as useless as a glass eye at a keyhole and will never make a dent in your sin-covered heart.

Harry Monroe stepped out and said, "Don't you men want to hear the story of men who used to be dips (pick-pockets), yeggs (safe-blowers), burglars, second-story workers, drunkards, and have done time in the big house, and who today are sober, honest, have good homes, and are trusted and respected; of women who used to sell their womanhood to whoever would buy, were slaves to dope and drink, and are now married and have children of their own? Come down to the mission and hear stories of redeemed lives that will stir you, no matter whether you have ever been inside of a church or have wandered away from God and decency."

I turned to the crowd that sat there with me, and said, "Boys, I bid the old life good-by." Some laughed, some smiled, some shrugged their shoulders, and some looked with mingled expressions of admiration and disgust. One fellow said, "All right, Billy, if that's the way you feel about it."

I went to the mission that evening and liked what I heard. I went back again and again, and one night I went forward and publicly accepted Christ as my Saviour. If the same floor is in that old building, I can show you the knot hole in the board upon which I knelt that dark and stormy night forty years ago. I have followed Jesus from that day to this every second, like the hound on the trail of the fox, and will continue until he leads me through the pearly gate into the presence of God and it closes on its jeweled hinges.

My Wife

When I joined the old White Sox, in 1883, the ball grounds were located on the lake front at the foot of Randolph, Washington and Madison streets, near where the Art Institute now stands. Later they were moved to the west side of the city, and in going from the grounds I always went north on Throop Street to the hotel where I boarded.

On the corner of Throop and Adams streets stood Jefferson Park Presbyterian Church. One Sunday evening I went there to attend Christian Endeavor meeting, and was introduced to a black-eyed, black-haired young lady, eighteen years old, named Helen Amelia Thompson. Her father was William Thompson, who at that time had the largest milk dairy and ice-cream establishment in the city. The family lived across the street from the church.

The first time I saw those flashing black eyes and dark hair and white teeth, I said to myself, "There's a swell girl." I always planned to attend that church and the young people's meetings whenever our club was playing in Chicago.

After several weeks I braced up one evening and asked Miss Thompson if I could see her home. She shied off for a minute, then smiled and said, "Yes," and from that time on I was hooked.

I used to attend prayer meetings and always sat on a row of seats along the wall where I could keep one eye on Neil, as everybody called her, and the other on the preacher. She had a fellow and tried to "team me up" with a girl chum of hers; but I didn't like the other girl. She had a camel-like neck, and humped over when she walked, liquid, gazelle-like eyes, was flat-footed and had a drawling, croony voice like Rudy Vallee's, and I passed her up as a pay car does a tramp.

I passed the Thompson home on my way to practice at ten o'clock in the morning, back to lunch at noon, back for the game in the afternoon, then home for supper. Nell used to time my goings and comings and would be out sweeping the front steps and the sidewalk. If we had an extra-long game, she swept on until I showed up. I would explain the game, who won or lost, how many hits and runs I made.

Finally, one time I went to see her—it was New Year's night, 1888. She had on an ox-blood cashmere dress, and a natural-colored lynx neckpiece thrown about her shoulders, which her parents had given her for Christmas, and which I had never seen before. Oh, boy! She was a knock-out! She looked like I imagine the Queen of Sheba did when she visited Solomon. She had ditched her beau, and I had given the gate to a girl I had out in Iowa. So I braced right up, just before midnight, and asked "Nell, will you marry me?" She came back at me so quick it almost floored me: "Yes, with all my heart."

I went home feeling as though I had wings on my feet. I didn't sleep that night. Visions of those black eyes stared at me from the darkness and turned night into day.

That spring I was sold to Pittsburgh; it was optional with me whether I went or not. A. G. Spalding and Cap Anson said, "Now, Billy, you can stay if you want to, but Pittsburgh will pay you a big increase in salary." So Nell and I talked it over and we decided it would be a good move for me to go, and I did. I had seven hundred dollars saved, and during that season up to the day we were married I saved twelve hundred dollars and sent it all to Nell to bank, and from then until now she has been my banker, bookkeeper, and pays all bills.

We have the old sofa in our home on which we used to "spark" and build our castles in the air, many of which have been crushed and lie in ruins at our feet, and some of which still stand, buttressed about by a love that blazes as brightly as it did when we plighted our eternal allegiance forty-three years ago.

I left the team in Indianapolis that evening after the game, and went to Chicago. We were married on September 5, 1888, by Dr. David C. Marquis, of McCormick Theological Seminary, of Chicago, at two o'clock in the afternoon. A. G. Spalding had a box draped for us at the ball grounds and had us come down there before we left for Pittsburgh.

The grandstand and bleachers arose and cheered us, and my old team-mates of the Chicagos all lined up in front of our box, and with hats off wished us happiness and long life. We left Chicago for Pittsburgh on the Pennsylvania Limited at five o'clock. That same train still runs, with the same number—old No. 2. Every time it passes through our home town, Winona Lake, Indiana, Ma and I say, "There goes our honey-moon train."

Players could take their wives with them on the swing around the circuit if they wished, but as salaries were not big and the trips were expensive, they did not often do so. Mrs. Sunday's parents were well-to-do for those days and paid her expenses so she was with me half the season.

When her father learned we were engaged, he "shelled the woods," declaring no daughter of his should every marry a ball player; but her mother, one of the noblest souls that ever breathed, was on our side, and of course "dad" had to surrender, which he did in July, and Nell wired me in Philadelphia: "Dad says it's all right." That afternoon I made three hits and had five put-outs.

Mrs. Sunday's father became my most loyal supporter, both as a ball player and as an evangelist. I played ball nearly four years after we were married. After I became an evangelist he always came to hear me preach. I suppose the fact that he was an old soldier, member of the 51st Illinois, and was severely wounded in the Battle of Shiloh, and that my own father was a member of the 23d Iowa, helped to establish a bond of sympathy; and then I was married to his favorite daughter, Nell. He joined Jefferson Park Presbyterian Church and was "mustered out" a Christian.